The
Secret Book
of
CIA Humor

The
Secret Book
of
CIA Humor

ED MICKOLUS

PELICAN PUBLISHING COMPANY
Gretna 2011

*The word "Pelican" and the depiction of a pelican are
trademarks of Pelican Publishing Company, Inc., and are
registered in the U.S. Patent and Trademark Office.*

Library of Congress Cataloging-in-Publication Data

Mickolus, Edward F.
  The secret book of CIA humor / by Ed Mickolus.
    p. cm.
  ISBN 978-1-58980-904-8 (pbk. : alk. paper) 1. Espionage—Humor. 2.
Espionage, American—Miscellanea. 3. United States. Central Intelligence
Agency. I. Title.
  PN6231.E75M53 2011
  818'.602—dc23
                              2011016870

Printed in the United States of America

Published by Pelican Publishing Company, Inc.
1000 Burmaster Street, Gretna, Louisiana 70053

All statements of fact, opinion, or analysis expressed are those of the author
and do not reflect the official positions or views of the CIA or any other U.S.
government agency. Nothing in the contents should be construed as asserting or
implying U.S. government authentication of information or Agency endorsement
of the author's views. This material has been reviewed by the CIA to prevent the
disclosure of classified information.

For the men and women of the Intelligence Community and the Spy-Fi humor heroes whose senses of humor get us all through the serious business of protecting our country.

☺ Life is a tragedy for those who feel and
a comedy for those who think. ☺

—My favorite fortune cookie

Table of Malcontents

Acknowledgments. 9

Introduction 11

Note on Abbreviations, Acronyms, and Other
Intentionally Confusing Terminology. 15

Shout Your Badge Number Down the Burn Chute 19

Fun with Phones. 41

A Funny Thing Happened on the Way to the
Ops Meeting 47

Battles with the Budget and the Budgeteers. 65

Homegrown Humor. 67

The Comedy Club. 75

The Memo Writers Strike Back 91

Understanding DO and DI Writing. 105

Humor as Political Indicator 111

Family Ties. 121

Security and Cover 123

Essays and Poems 131

DCI Humor. 151

The Hunt for Red October. 161

Writing Under PAR. 191
Aerial Surveillance and Other Air Stories 207
O'Toole's. 217
Miscellany 227
Further Reading 239
Epilogue 240

Acknowledgements

A special salute, to Danny Biederman, curator of the Spy-Fi Archives, and then in no particular order, to Spy-Fi heroes Chevy Chase as Emmett Fitz-Hume and Dan Aykroyd as Austin Millbarge (*Spies Like Us*), Red Buttons as Henry Wadsworth Phyfe (*The Double Life of Henry Phyfe*), Tom Adams as Charles Vine (*Second Best Secret Agent in the Whole Wide World*), Robert Vaughn as Napoleon Solo, David McCallum as Illya Kuryakin and Leo G. Carroll as Alexander Waverly (*The Man from U.N.C.L.E.*), James Coburn as Derek Flint (*Our Man Flint* and *In Like Flint*), Rowan Atkinson as Johnny English (*Johnny English*), Lando Buzzanca as James Tont (*James Tont: Operation Goldsinger*), Robert Culp as Kelly Robinson and Bill Cosby as Alexander Scott (*I Spy*), David Niven as Sir James Bond 007, Woody Allen as Jimmy Bond, and Peter Sellers as Evelyn Tremble (*Casino Royale*), James Bond in all incarnations, Patrick McGoohan as John Drake (*Secret Agent*), Zachary Levi as Charles Bartowski, Yvonne Strahovski as Sarah Walker, and Adam Baldwin as Colonel John Casey (*Chuck*), Dean Martin as Matt Helm (*The Silencers, The Wrecking Crew,* and *Murderers' Row, The Ambushers*), Alec Guinness as James Wormold (*Our Man in Havana*), Rowan Atkinson as Nigel Small-Fawcett (*Never Say Never Again*), Patrick Macnee as John Steed and Diana Rigg as Mrs. Emma Peel (*The Avengers*), Frankie Avalon as Craig Gamble (*Dr. Goldfoot*), Don Adams (Steve Carell in the

2008 film) as Maxwell Smart and Barbara Feldon (Anne Hathaway in the 2008 film) as Agent 99 (*Get Smart*), and Mike Myers as Austin Powers (*International Man of Mystery, The Spy Who Shagged Me,* and *Goldmember*).

Introduction

What members of the Intelligence Community do for our country, what they're like, and what they like are often shrouded in mystery and misunderstanding to the general public, fostered by inaccurate depictions of the IC in popular culture, including Hollywood movies and television series, novels, the news media, the blognoscenti, punditocracy, commentariat, and others who claim to be experts because they could follow the plot of *24* without hitting "rewind." If you Google "CIA humor," you'll get hundreds of thousands of hits, but essentially only two jokes. The first joke making the pixel rounds goes like this:

The CIA advertised for an assassin position, GS-13, no experience necessary. Two men and a woman applied for the position. They were taken into a room and told that if they wanted the job, they would have to go into the next room and kill whoever was in that room. They all agreed. The first man was handed a gun and ushered through door number one. Inside he found his wife, bound, gagged, and sitting on a chair. After a minute, he came out of the room and told his supervisor that he could not kill her. The supervisor said, "Get out of here, and quit wasting my time." The supervisor turned to man number two. He handed him the gun and told him to walk into room number two. The applicant complied, where he found *his* wife, bound, gagged, and sitting in a chair. He walked over, held the gun to her head, cocked the trigger, waited two minutes, but then broke down crying. When he came out of the room, crying, saying he just couldn't do it, the supervisor said, "You're a disgrace and you, too, need to get out of here." He handed the gun to the third applicant, a woman, and sent her into room number three. She did so, and saw her husband, bound, gagged, and sitting in a chair. After ten seconds, the supervisor heard three shots, followed by silence, then banging, yelling, screaming and then silence again. When the woman walked out of the room, the supervisor asked her what had happened. She replied, "I walked over and held the gun to his head and fired three times. But when I found out I was only shooting blanks, I had to break the chair and beat him to death."

Great joke, but dead (you'll excuse the pun) wrong about what intelligence officers do for a living. I could tell you the second one, but then I'd have to kill you. Alas, that lame quip *is* the second joke!

This book is designed to give you a flavor of what real intelligence officers are all about, as illustrated by the humorous stories they tell about themselves, the pranks and practical jokes they pull on each other, the urban legends they tell, and the humorous situations they have experienced based upon their unique profession. Our sense of humor is far more extensive than the occasional throwaway tossed out by James Bond. The book adds to the stories told by Tom Sileo in his *CIA Humor* (Alexandria : Washington House/ Trident Media, 2004) and the late Roger Hall's 1957 classic on his experiences with the WWII-era Office of Strategic Services, the CIA predecessor, a book at long last back in print.

Although James Bond routinely saved the world by himself rather than working in a team, members of the Intelligence Community get things done by relying on each other. Although most of the stories come from my colleagues in the CIA, where I was honored to serve for thirty-three plus years, this collection also reflects contributions of numerous other members of the Intelligence Community. This book project was a typical IC team effort, drawing upon the input of scores of members of the extended Agency family, as well as intelligence officers in other U.S. intelligence agencies, currently serving or retired, who provided their stories. Many of them still toil under cover, or are congenitally allergic to publicity, so while I would like to give them the recognition for their sacrifices—and their humor—that they so richly deserve, I'll abide by their wishes.

A few contributors, however, do not have the burden of cover. Among them are the officers, newsletter editors, and members of the Association for Intelligence Officers (AFIO) and the Central Intelligence Agency Retirees Association, who came to the rescue when I ran out of material. Jan Goldman, editor of the Scarecrow Professional Intelligence Education Series (S.P.I.E.S.), encouraged me every step of the way, and graciously added a few of his jokes from his Defense Intelligence Agency colleagues. Chris Wright, from the Marine Corps Intelligence Activity, provided several loopy letters from a perplexed public. Memories of Air America are courtesy of Charles M. Griffith, acting station manager at Danang and Nharang, Vietnam, and station manager at Savannakhet, Laos. I was especially honored to be contacted by retired Army Lt. Col. Greg Hutchison, ninety-eight, who offered his experiences before the CIA opened for business. Additional contributions came from Sgt. Mike Pafford, USAF, 6924th Security Squadron (USAFSS); former Directorate of Intelligence analyst Robert W. Pringle, now of the University of Kentucky and the Virginia Military Institute; Mark Jensen of the Office of the Director of National Intelligence; former DOD country director, AFIO member, and contributing editor to the *Intelligencer* Dwayne Anderson; Bill B.; Karl Broom; David Bush; Kevin C.; Brian Detrick; Fritz Ermarth; Laurie Gourlay; Keith Hall; Paul K. (I know who he is; he knows who he is; you don't need to know who he is); Julian Nall; Lou Palumbo; Bob P.; Lewis Regenstein (who had to resign because he could never tell when he had run out of invisible ink); Greg S.; Herbert Saunders; Lily Smith; and Linda Winner. Janice Sebring authored *The Hunt for*

Red October: The Untold Story. Former Principal Deputy for Human Resources Tom McCluskey is a wealth of stories and writes a pretty moving song, too. My thanks also go to ace joke-writers Michael Bohumil, John Shultis, Kathleen Allyn, and Pamela Haeberer.

This book would truly not have been possible—at least, not without me breaking several statutes—without the contribution of the Agency's Publications Review Board, who has assisted me in more than a dozen book publication projects in ensuring that I do not inadvertently blurt out classified information. The PRB team can always be counted upon to do its usually thankless task with grace, thoroughness, speed, patience, and in this case especially, exceptionally good humor.

To keep the book in the same "voice," I have often kept the first person narrative setup of the jokes sent in by others. Although I had a wide-ranging career, it wasn't *that* wide-ranging, and not all of these situations happened to me.

And just to be clear, no secrets were harmed in the making of this book.

If you would like to contribute your espionage humor to sequels of this book, please send them to Ed Mickolus c/o Pelican Publishing Company, 1000 Burmaster St. Gretna, LA 70053. Please indicate whether you wish public attribution, or would like to remain anonymous. And with some of the jokes we've received, we quite understand why you don't want to be known.

Note on Abbreviations, Acronyms, and Other Intentionally Confusing Terminology

Acronyms and their linguistic cousins are the lifeblood of the Intelligence Community, designed to inform those in the circle of trust while obfuscating to those deemed lacking the need to know. All mentions of offices, etc., in this book refer to CIA-specific items, except where noted. A few of the more common abbreviations and terms used in this book include:

Box: In operations, the noun or verb form of "polygraph"; In the Directorate of Intelligence, a supplemental, short article tangential to a main, finished intelligence product, such as a *President's Daily Brief* narrative

CIA: Central Intelligence Agency

COB: Depending upon context, Close of Business or Chief of Base

COPS: Chief of Operations, usually the third-ranking officer in a station or headquarters component

COS: Depending upon context, Chief of Station or Chief of Staff

DA: CIA's Directorate of Administration (it is now known as the Directorate of Support)

DI: CIA's Directorate of Intelligence (for a brief period, it was known as the National Foreign Assessment Center), where the analysts work

DIA: Defense Intelligence Agency

DNI: Director of National Intelligence

DO: CIA's Directorate of Operations (in its history, it has also been called the Deputy Directorate of Operations, the Directorate of Plans, the Deputy Directorate of Plans, and the National Clandestine Service), which runs espionage collection operations

DS&T: CIA's Directorate of Science and Technology, not to be confused with the DST, a French intelligence service

EOD: Entry on Duty. Can refer to the date when a rookie actually shows up for his/her first day of work, or to the rookie him/herself; The duration of one's EOD-hood is indeterminate, although its most extreme delimiter is the date of the individual's first promotion

EPA: Exceptional Performance Award

FBI: Federal Bureau of Investigation

FBIS: Foreign Broadcast Information Service, renamed the Open Source Center and transferred to the Office of the Directorate of National Intelligence when the DNI was created

FNU: First Name Unknown

FNU LNU: First Name and Last Name Unknown; also the name of an Agency softball team I coached

Hall File: One's reputation, which is not written down anywhere, but is vital to one's assignments and promotions

Hard cover: In the Directorate of Intelligence, a substantive research paper of indeterminate length, but longer than a typical one-page current intelligence piece

HUMINT: Human source intelligence

IA: Intelligence analyst, intelligence assistant, or Intelligence Appraisal, depending upon context

IM: Intelligence Memorandum

LDA: Office of Leadership Analysis

LNU: Last Name Unknown

NBCD: The former Nuclear, Biological, and Chemical Weapons Division

NFAC: National Foreign Assessment Center (an alias used for a brief period by the Directorate of Intelligence)

NGA: National Geospatial Intelligence Agency (its predecessors include NPIC—the National Photographic Interpretation Center; NIMA—the National Imagery and Mapping Agency; and eight other agencies)

NHB: New Headquarters Building of the CIA campus in Langley, Virginia

NID: National Intelligence Daily

NIE: National Intelligence Estimate

NPC: Nonproliferation Center

NRO: National Reconnaissance Office

NSA: National Security Agency

OHB: Original Headquarters Building of CIA, often incorrectly called the Old Headquarters Building

OL: CIA's Office of Logistics

OMS: CIA's Office of Medical Services

ONE: The CIA's defunct Office of National Estimates

OPA: Depending upon the era, the DI's 1980s-era Office of Political Analysis, or the mid-1990s-2000s Office of Public Affairs

OSWR: Office of Scientific and Weapons Research

OWTP: A former DI office that covered weapons and technological programs, but was commonly referred to as the Office of Wet Toilet Paper

PDB: President's Daily Brief

PCS: Permanent Change of Station—Switching from one duty assignment to another, usually in the field

PFBLOOPER/1: Operational nickname for an agent, instead of using his true name in correspondence that might be leaked

PHOTINT: Photographic intelligence

Ref: Reference—a previous cable cited in another cable; Similar to footnoting.

RP: Research Paper, a longer form of finished intelligence in the Directorate of Intelligence

RUMINT: Rumor intelligence—Not technically an official term, but widely cited; Also known as corridor radio

SAFE: Support for the Analyst File Environment, an early DI-wide cable delivery system

SEIB: Senior Executive Intelligence Brief, the successor to the *National Intelligence Daily*

Seventh Floor: Where the preponderance of the senior management of the CIA resides

SIS: Depending upon context, Senior Intelligence Service—the CIA's seniormost officers, or the British foreign intelligence service

SOVA: Office of Soviet Analysis

SPO: Security Protective Officer, the Agency's police force, also known as the Security Protective Service

Style Guide: Also known as the *DI Style Guide,* the analyst's equivalent of Strunk and White

TDY: Temporary Duty, and known as travel time; This can range from one day to 364 days

Trace: A biographic profile written on an individual who may be of operational interest

USG: United States Government

WMD: Weapons of Mass Destruction, usually including nuclear, radiological, chemical, and biological weapons and missile delivery systems

Shout Your Badge Number Down the Burn Chute:

Urban Legends, Capers, Practical Jokes, and Pranks

Part of any organization's esprit de corps *is the corpus of "war stories" passed from one generation to another. Although an organization's senior management generally prefers that this lore be confined to morally uplifting stories of how the organization's members handled the key substantive challenges facing it, these stories also reflect the "personality" of the organization in how its members release tension through creative use of humor.*

While I was involved with internal communication with CIA, I often tracked down oddball stories that make up this latter class of Agency lore. Some stories are Agency-specific urban legends—stories that have a moral to them, that are universally believed because they happened to a friend of a friend (FOAF; there's actually a scholarly journal called FOAFTales*), but upon research have been established to be, at best, hopelessly garbled digressions from the truth. Some, which sound like urban legends because of their implausibility, turn out to be true (the "truth is stranger than fiction" category). Of the latter, some are official actions, and others are nonofficial practical jokes pulled on individuals or on the Agency as a whole.*

The following, many of them told in first-person, are stories offered by dozens of Agency employees who requested anonymity. (I alerted everyone in my office to never let any of these people near my desk!) In cases in which it is possible, I have attempted to determine their veracity. Others do not permit such research, but are too hilarious not to include.

Welcome to the Agency

Rookies are often the targets of practical jokes. This Agency equivalent of good-natured fraternity hazing lets the new employee know that they have been accepted into the fold. One common story has the employee take his classified trash, inside a securely stapled "burn bag" to a chute, where the classified material is collected for destruction. The rookie is told that he is to shout the number of his badge—his unique identifier that Agency employees wear in all Agency buildings—down the burn chute so that a record can be kept of who made the decision to destroy the classified materials. Rare is the individual who admits to having actually complied with this instruction. (Similarly, I have yet to find a rookie willing to purchase Agency Prom tickets.) Others encourage rookies (known in the Agency as EODs for Entry on Duty) to shout their badge numbers into the toilet as they flush. Still others have EODs hold their badge before a nonexistent electronic reader supposedly hooked up next to the burn chute. Still others have rookies hold their badge toward any fixture on the ceiling (fire alarms, motion sensors, smoke detectors, etc., are fine) and yell "(badge number) reporting for duty!"

Some veterans of the National Photographic Interpretation Center (NPIC) were even more aggressive with this theme, telling the new guy that he had to clip his badge to the burn bag before he sent it down the chute so that the "guys at the bottom would know whom to contact if something had been improperly disposed of." After the rookies figured out that we were pulling their leg with the "clipping the badge on the bag" routine, we admitted that, in fact, you only had to yell your badge number down the chute, which usually fooled them for another few days. I remember walking down the hall of the NPIC building, hearing a badge number being yelled, and maybe giving a wink to the "old hand" standing next to the new guy.

By the way, despite extensive efforts to track down the story,

I found no one who ever actually slid down a burn chute, notwithstanding elaborate legends of using rappelling equipment, burn bags as toboggans, etc.

A variation on this theme was practiced in the Directorate of Intelligence, in which an old hand was tasked with showing the EOD how to dispose of hundreds of sensitive documents and dissemination sheets. He proceeded to complain to the rookie about the amazingly absurd practices we go through: tear the first three pages of your control documents, write your badge number, employee number, date, and "destroyed" on the fourth sheet, then take the secretary's ink pad and place your thumb print on the fifth sheet. A horrified secretary berated our prankster when she discovered a phalanx of EODs with shiny, blackened hands.

Speaking of badges, which have a photo of the individual on its front, the story goes that a KGB officer infiltrated the Agency to study its sociology. Back home from his mission, he was asked what he'd learned. "Well, commissar, they are very religious, much more so that we expected." "How do you mean, comrade?" "Well, commissar, they all wear these icons around their necks. When they greet each other, they bow to each other, grab each other's icon in reverence, and intone 'Jesus Christ, is that *you*?!'"

NPIC officers sent EODs to the supply room to ask for a "cloud-eradicator pen" so that we could see all of the activity on the satellite image and not just what was in the cloud-free sections. Their confreres in the Printing Plant would ask new hires to obtain a "paper stretcher" and a bottle of half-tone dots. At the Pentagon, rookies are asked to go get an ID Ten Tango form (ID 10 T).

Senior officials are not immune to initiation rites. In 1977, the new director of an office arrived from his senior position in the private sector. He chose the unfortunate date of April 1 to have his first Headquarters staff meeting and informed his secretary that he would not arrive until 9:30 am, giving us just enough time to set up his welcome. Awaiting on his desk was an "Eyes Only" envelope with a memo to him entitled "Letter of Involuntary Separation" that went on to explain that for Agency culture, firing offenses included excessive tardiness—an indication of lack of motivation and not taking the job seriously in an environment that routinely assumes that employee work long hours. The final paragraph read something like "Good luck finding a new job, turkey." My job was to forge the rather distinctive signature of the Director of Personnel. Our victim took it as a fun prank, but sadly for me, he realized after only being here for three weeks that I must have been involved. I never did learn to live my cover well.

Speaking of turkeys, Thanksgiving 1996 greeted new hires with a faked *What's News at CIA* (the Agency's internal newsletter) on the DCI's annual turkey giveaway. One newbie checked with his branch chief, who assured him that the turkey came out of Employee Activity Association coffers so that there would be no conflict over improper use of funds. If the rookie could not use the turkey, he should still pick it up, and the branch chief's wife would give it to a local charity. Other analysts chimed in with their support of the program, fondly remembering receiving "a good-size bird." Others complained that this was a fairly new program, and that *they* had not been able to benefit in their first year. Encouraged by this apparent act of corporate benevolence, the rookie shared this message with fellow EODs. Although he could not use the turkey himself, he saw an opportunity of getting on the good side of the boss by donating it to the boss's wife. The EODs thus set off to an unfamiliar part of the building, somewhere in the basement on the other side of the compound. Once in the general area, he sought out a uniformed security officer for directions to the room. The security officer pointed down a very long, barren hallway. At the end of this pilgrimage, the rookie found that GD39 is the address of the furthermost burn chute. History does not record whether he yelled his badge number or something more appropriate, albeit heartfelt and colorful.

An I hope apocryphal variant of this story sends the rookie to the DCI's office, whereupon the rookie asks the Director's secretary "Where's the turkey?" and is admonished that the Director is very sensitive to being called that, being Greek and all . . .

Food Fights

A Directorate of Operations Division Chief had just completed his annual physical. A co-worker, posing as an Office of Medical Services doctor, called and told him he had a rare blood disease for which the only known cure was to coat his stomach with chocolate milk. For about six weeks, the Division Chief diligently drank his chocolate milk eight times a day and was often seen walking down the hall with a greenish tinge to his face, because the poor man couldn't stand milk, much less chocolate milk. It was only when he reported in to the medics for his post-treatment screening that he discovered he'd been had!

A noted analyst chocoholic was not shy about reminding people how many shopping days were left until her birthday. One year, colleagues gave her little refrigerator magnets shaped like Hershey miniatures. After they had held her memos in place for a few months, we replaced them one night with real Hershey miniatures with little magnets glued to them. The elusive smell of chocolate maddened her for a few weeks until we owned up.

One year, the Director of Central Intelligence decreed that there was to be no—repeat—no alcohol served at the annual holiday parties. There were some winks and nods, however, and various confederates on the seventh floor called each office to warn when the big wheels were en route to the parties. In one Directorate of Operations division, the punch bowl was hidden under the deputy chief's desk on the seat of his chair. Before the bowl could be moved back to the party table, the deputy backed into his chair and sat right in the punch bowl!

At the 1983 retirement luncheon of a colleague who had been a black bag man, after we placed our orders, I had the waitress bring him a plate with a bottle of Aunt Jemima and a pack of Kleenex on it. He had to open the sealed envelope to find he had been served an appropriate dish: a syrup/tissues entrée. (The editor apologizes to our readers for this atrocious pun.)

On April Fool's Day, an analyst brought in Oreos with toothpaste for filling instead of the usual vanilla cream filling. A small group of more senior analysts ate most of the box that afternoon with only a comment that the Oreos tasted funny.

Wake Up Calls and Sophomoric Soporifics

My Career Training class was divided into two sections, each of which had an individual who would editorialize on the occasional less-than-fascinating presentation on accounting practices by falling asleep. Our class would run pools as to which individual would fall asleep first, and when. It was a major point of honor for our class's section to win the day's competition. And it kept the rest of us awake!

DCI Woolsey was scheduled to brief on the Hill, with a retinue from the Office of Congressional Affairs in tow. It was a slow news day, even for C-SPAN, which decided to run his hearings live. It was a small, cramped room with air conditioning that had seen better days, and by the start of the fourth hour of his testimony, sans breaks, one of his OCA handlers was heroically battling sleepiness. He tried desperately to keep his chin up, literally, but it, and his eyelids, kept sinking down. Unfortunately, the faithful retainer was sitting directly behind Woolsey, in the camera frame for the world to see. (OK, C-SPAN isn't high up in the Nielsen ratings, but it still presented a problem.) His buddies back at OCA Headquarters saw what was happening on their TV monitors, and decided to help him out. They sent a page to him that read "ZZZZZZZZ." When the page vibration went off, it shocked him awake, and he jumped up, to the applause of his viewing audience.

(Director of National Intelligence Mike McConnell agrees on the perils of testifying before the Hill. In reviewing his forty years of service, he observed "Except for a few days testifying on the Hill, I wouldn't trade a single day of it.")

You Call this Art? Beauty in the Eye of the Beholder

After taking a data set and visualizing it (converting the data values to a color index and printing a picture), we learned that the employee art show was coming up. So we put the picture in a truly hideous pink frame, and we bet our branch chief that we would enter it into the show and if it got a ribbon, he'd have to take us all out to lunch. He took the bet, believing there was no way it would win. Keep in mind, we didn't bet for first place, but for *any* ribbon.

The picture was proudly displayed in the art exhibit and at the end of the month we discovered that there were *no* awards—it was a showing and not a competition. Because this fact hurt our chances at our free lunch, we promptly went out to a local trophy shop and bought two ribbons: one for fourth place and one for honorable mention. We awarded the picture fourth place overall for the show and an honorable mention for creative media.

We never specified that the Fine Arts Commission had to award the picture a prize, just that it would win a ribbon. Our awarding it had no bearing on the bet (not that we pointed out to our branch chief this possible area of contention).

"Ambient Internal Waves in Spring" can still be viewed in the office of a National Reconnaissance Office analyst.

You Call This Art? The Sequel

Many Agency officers, after looking at the huge Washington Color School paintings that grace the hallways of the Headquarters Buildings, suggest that "my four-year-old could do better" or "you could fling paint at a canvas and do better." Inspired by these exhortations, analysts in the Office of Scientific and Weapons

Research decided to test this theory. One day, they brought to the Front Office a medium-sized canvas, several buckets of paint, and several brushes, with a sign asking passers-by to flip a few dabs of paint randomly on the canvas as they proceeded to their meetings. After a few weeks, the canvas was covered in streaks of paint and ready for exhibit. The ringleaders found a spot for the "Disturbed Analyst" masterpiece in the Headquarters Atrium hallway, where it hung untouched for months. One day, the Fine Arts Commission decided that this unrecorded acquisition should nonetheless be treated like the other art, and had it roped and stanchioned. When the Atrium was renovated, it was carefully taken down, catalogued, and hung elsewhere. Eventually, word of the story behind the painting leaked. You can still visit it in the successor component's front office.

Signs of the Times

Agency officers often figured that technological breakthroughs made by the US would eventually make it to the Soviet Union's repertoire, either through parallel development or through outright theft of intellectual property. This assumption extended to intelligence collection methods. They reasoned that the Soviets would eventually develop an overhead satellite capability that would permit the USSR to take images of CIA Headquarters. During a period of heightened tensions during the Cold War, several analysts of matters-Soviet decided to test the capability of the opposition's overhead systems by unfurling a bed sheet from the Headquarters roof that read "F*** COMMUNISM!"

Several employees were taken aback by the proliferation of signs on easels that greeted them at Headquarters entrances. One day, a team placed five small signs in front of the official signs that read:

All these signs
Of our times
Clutter up

Our egress lines
Burma Shave

Posted over several burn chute doors was the sign:
    You Have Been Exposed
    To Classified Material
    Destroy Yourself Before
    Leaving The Building

Word to the wise: be sure to check your whereabouts, even with signage. Several wags set up static surveillance sites to watch the fun after they switched the signs to the men's and women's rest rooms.

Some days after the completion of the Headquarters cafeteria's mezzanine, a sign appeared chastising those who had mistaken it for a platform-diving area.

After hearing numerous "who's that?" comments about senior officials at Agencywide gatherings, the Agency Information Staff (which handles internal communications) posted a set of 8 x 10 glossy photos of the Agency's senior managers in the first floor corridors. During the night, someone else placed a votive candle in front of the photos.

The Agency Portrait Gallery features large paintings of the former Directors of Central Intelligence. A DCI's portrait is painted only when the Director's term of service ends. Word in the hallways was that DCIs started to worry when they saw the official portraitist, armed with easel and palette, asking to get on the Director's calendar.

When former JFK speechwriter Ted Sorenson withdrew as a candidate for DCI during the Senate confirmation process, someone scrawled a stick figure sketch of Sorenson on an 8 x 10 sheet of paper and taped it at the end of the portrait gallery.

After a multimillion dollar satellite exploded in 1998, a "You break it, you buy it" sign appeared in the DS&T front office.

This Really Happened to the Gardener of the Cousin of My Branch Chief a Couple of Years Ago

Numerous posters to Agency computer bulletin boards, discussion groups, blogs, wikis, and listservs believe that all sorts of unfortunate fates will befall anyone who posts the complete name of any major American newspaper. Postings are thus replete with references to the *W********* P*** and N** Y*** T****. Alas, it's all an urban (if not urbane) legend.

Sounds Like an Urban Legend, But This One's True

When the hallway connecting the Original and New Headquarters Buildings was complete, the General Services Administration team reported to the New Building Project Manager that the construction had trapped a bulldozer in the cafeteria courtyard. Possible solutions—including demolishing enough of the glass walls and hiring a crane to get it out—cost more than the value of the bulldozer. So after a suitable memorial service, the bulldozer was buried in the courtyard. Alas, there is no marker commemorating this event.

The Techies Strike Back

I once gave a colleague a parting gift from the old Office of Global Issues terrorism and narcotics shop—a particularly realistic time-bomb clock. SPOs responding to a malfunctioning alarm in his vault one night found it and called him about it. He reassured them that it was only a decoration. I gave out several other less-realistic devices later.

In a grab for his fifteen minutes of fame, a DO officer consented to be interviewed on national television news regarding his non-Agency activities. Our audio staff superimposed faked prompts to his answers, leading to hilarious results.

Back in the Jurassic age (before personal computers), we used Frieden calculators, an electro-mechanical contraption, for all of our calculations. These devices worked with a series of gears and cranks, and were especially loud when dealing with large numbers. We discovered that one particular computation would set it off on a longish do-loop that generated an almost musical series of notes. The twelve of us in our branch each programmed our calculators for the same computation, then set them off to play as a sequential "round" to greet our long-suffering branch chief.

Never Leave Your Desk Unattended

Our office has one of the Agency's legendary paramilitary officers, who comes to us replete with stories of machine gun battles on his front lawn, martial arts trophies galore, and lots of machismo. When he returned from leave, he discovered that his office had been redecorated with tasteful pink ribbon and lace curtains and doilies.

Vaseline is a wonderful product, which can be put to good use on a PC's power button, file drawers, seat buttons, the handle of the refrigerator, etc. Just make sure that you also put a big dab of it on your victim's top few tissues, the cleaning spray can's button, and other cleaning items, too.

One major computer manufacturer ships computers using about three cubic feet of box space per cubic inch of material shipped. One night after installing about thirty new computers, we took the boxes and stacked them up in our boss's office. From floor to ceiling, the entire office was filled, except for enough space to open the door and have it barely clear the first row of cardboard. Of course, we also superglued his pens and pencils to his desk tray, and used the megastapler to affix a ream of paper to his blotter, binders, and in-box. We included a few simple "gimme" pranks: leaving the 3-ring binders open on his shelf, awaiting him to pull out one of these time-delay jokes. Not satisfied with these warm-up gags, the team returned weeks later to hammer a set of in-boxes together, making a tower of in-boxes that required them to open the drop ceiling in the boss's office.

Make sure to *always* lock your computer when you walk away for even a minute. One office took a screen shot of the boss's desktop, made that picture the computer's background, and moved all of his icons into a temporary folder. Upon returning, the branch chief discovered that he couldn't click on anything on his desktop.

Suitably chastened, he learned to lock his computer. However, his staff put a post-it note on the bottom of his mouse (this works only with an optical/laser mouse), making him think the mouse didn't work.

His staff later changed his screen to display black characters on a black background.

Another time, they put his PC in an endless loop of Jeopardy, which morphed into looking like it was erasing his C: drive, followed by a "Gotcha!" banner.

The boss was getting married at the end of the week (which is really what had inspired us anyway) and with the additional stress of our shenanigans, he decided to have his door combination changed to keep us out. So we got into the room on the other side of the wall one day, and, going through the ceiling, we filled his office with balloons, from the floor to about waist level. Needless to say, he was pretty pleased with us.

A particularly fastidious and meticulous DI analyst (renowned for washing his car keys in the dishwasher) made the error of leaving his watch on his desk. His officemates set it ahead one hour, making sure to also change the time on the office clocks. Panicking at the time, he ran off to pick up his child from his $1/minute-late charging daycare center. Hearing the real time on his radio, he called his office from the Toll Road to explain what had happened, to be greeted with a chorus of "What time is it, John?" from his officemates. Not to let a good joke die, his officemates reset the office clocks fifteen minutes ahead, then watched their foil leave for lunch fifteen minutes early each day, a victim of conditioned response. (We ended his car keys-dishwasher habit by freezing his keys in a block of ice in the refrigerator.)

One prankster team grabs badges left on colleagues' desks, photocopies them, and returns them to the desk, with the photos to be used later in Photoshop-assisted forgeries. Among their best work are desk photos of family members, with the names of colleagues superimposed over those of one's spouse, children, and the family dog. It sometimes takes months for the victim to notice. One variation included a sheep in the wedding photo. Upon removing the sheep photo, the victim found that the photo of another woman had been placed underneath the sheep photo.

Our practical jokers used another badge photo to create bumper stickers with "I (heart sign) Gary," which were distributed throughout the cubicles. Gary stormed in to the branch chief's office to complain. Closing the door to her office to counsel poor Gary, she discovered that the pranksters had superimposed Gary's face on her life size poster of Washington Bullets 7'7" center Manute Bol.

Despite frequent reminders by Security officers that one should always password-protect one's computer when leaving, some people never believe that it applies to them. If moles don't get them, pranksters will. Upon returning to their terminals, such scofflaws have found:

- On bootup, the sound card plays the *When Harry Met Sally* faked orgasm sound sample at high volume, to the delight of the rest of the cubicle dwellers.
- On bootup, the terminal displays the message "Just *what* do you think you're doing."
- The terminal had been used to send faked e-mails to a colleague he was socially interested in. The series of e-mail tennis had gotten increasingly amorous, and required some serious 'splainin' on his part. (Footnote: The couple dated twice. Nothing came of it.)

- The terminal had been used to send a faked e-mail to the boss indicating that "It's time I came out of the closet, and I need your thought on how I do this." Of course, the message was sent only after the foil returned to his desk and hit the "enter" key, thereby sending the message himself.
- The PC was giving the user (false) messages warning that it was erasing the C: drive.
- The S e-mail command had been reprogrammed from "Save" to "Send."
- A large "GOTCHA" banner was scrolling across the screen.
- The display had been changed to black characters on a black background.
- The keyboard had been remapped, with everything shifted over one space to the right.
- The . and , had been swapped.

A nearsighted branch chief returned to his office to discover that some unidentifiable item had been placed on top of the clock on his office wall, out of his reach (and sight). His charges mumbled something about "motion detector," satisfying the branch chief's curiosity. The Twinkie stayed on his clock for months.

One of our victims couldn't figure out why his computer was always breaking down whereas everyone else's ran perfectly. Little did he know that we swiped parts from his computer to fix everyone else's malfunctioning systems.

A branch chief was particularly proud of a "celestial sphere" sculpture he had hung in his office. The next day, he discovered that his branch members had cut fish out of the covers of the office's serial publication, and had attached these goldfish to the inside of the sphere. In a classic misdirection operation, the miscreants created the cutouts in the deputy's office, leaving the trash cuttings for the branch chief to discover.

An analyst irritated the rest of the branch by filling up the office's refrigerator with case upon case of his specialty no salt/ caffeine colas, leaving no space for the rest of them. Our pranksters would grab a cola can at random and shake it, then put it back in the fridge. The explosion wouldn't necessarily go off that day, and could take months, but an eventual *Whoosh!* and shriek would indicate "Mission Accomplished!"

As a farewell gift to one of our colleagues who went on rotation to NSA, we snuck into his new office and hid an egg (which we had perforated) in the back of his conservafile; it would take perhaps three weeks for this to start smelling. We hid chicken bones further up the conservafile as a cover for the egg smell. Sure enough, this time bomb went off in three weeks, and I got an irate call from him, claiming that I had hidden the food there. My reply? "Which came first, the chicken or the egg?"

While we were serving as duty officers in the White House Situation Room, we noticed that one of the staff took particular pride in the finish on the conference room table. He'd spend uncounted hours carefully waxing and polishing every square inch of that table until it had a mirror finish. But every night, he'd look at the table and see little circular spots all over it. So he'd go back to polishing it again. He never did discover that we'd put a portable ping-pong net on it when he'd leave and play tournaments during quiet times.

Even if you're at your desk, pranksters can strike. One colleague carried two Kleenexes, would do a fake nose-blow into one and then throw a putatively used one into a cubicle, where the cube-dweller ducked beneath his desk.

Moving Experiences: Packouts, TDYs, and Office Moves

I was in the midst of an overseas packout, moving all of my household effects, when one of the local packers came and asked me to check the crate for the horse. They had constructed a huge wooden crate, complete with breathing holes, and were ready to encase our horse for shipment! After taking a minute to absorb all of this, I then realized that I had not seen the dog in quite awhile. He greeted my subsequent calls with a muffled woof. Yep, he'd already been packed! When uncrated, he lunged at the first local he saw!

At another post, it can never be said that the packers weren't thorough. When unpacking here in the States following a tour in Africa, I found that all of the kitchen trash had been packed, including a four-foot-long snake, pronounced DOA.

One colleague left his garment bag on a coat rack, which his local pranksters noticed. They filled it with steel rods purloined from cubicle partitions. Although he observed that it seemed a little heavier than normal, he was on a tight deadline, so he ran off without checking. It was checked for him, when the metal detector went off at the airport. Although he got through after some explaining, he was trapped into carrying the rods with him, because it was official government property which he had to protect.

The same individual left his gym bag in eyeshot of the pranksters, who swiped his socks and underwear, put them in the freezer, then replaced them just in time for him to walk to the gym.

He wasn't done, though. He brought his suitcase to his office, where it was promptly filled with paperclips.

No matter where you work, one individual is always the last to know the latest developments, be it in the world or just office gossip/politics. Taking advantage of this, one day I sent an officewide e-mail announcing a farewell party for our foil (who wasn't scheduled to go anywhere). I then watched a parade of colleagues stop by to wish our befuddled friend well in his next job, which he was hard pressed to identify to his curious interlocutors.

Back in the golden age of working in OHB, a pneumatic tube system was used to coordinate cables, share drafts, and at times send hardcopy background material, etc. It was also excellent for sending surprises to various offices. Cable Secretariat once received a sparrow.

One of the legendary clandestine Agency newsletters was a serial publication found at the coffee machine in the DI's Office of Russian and Eurasian Analysis, spoofing Tom Clancy's *The Hunt for Red October* as if it was covered by the *National Intelligence Daily* (see a later chapter for a copy. Of *The Hunt,* not of the *NID!*). As of this writing, Jack Ryan is still stuck in coordination hassles.

Not to be outdone, while waiting for what seemed an interminable period for several layers of the bureaucracy to bless their efforts, the Human Resources Oversight Council's Program Office (HROC-PO) announced that it had gone on strike as of June 10, 1997. Celebrating this diversion into unionization of Agency workers, HROC published twenty-six editions of *The Daily Striker* (motto: It's News to Us!) during the 462-day crisis.

Fraternization

Romances within offices and across Directorates are commonplace in the Agency. Although there is always the problem of potential sexual harassment suits by those who believe that co-worker fraternization creates a hostile environment, most co-workers welcome their colleagues' good fortune. It makes carpooling easier, and at least you can talk about work with your cleared spouse. Many of these romances lead to marriages and are celebrated each Valentine's Day in the Agency's newsletter's article "How we became tandem couples."

But these romances also leave the participants open to practical jokes, such as the following:

In the early 1970s, our branch chief was a divorced middle-aged man who had a close personal relationship with one of his female analysts. They later were married. At the time of the story, however, they were just "good friends" who had a particular habit. Every day, the female analyst would come to work about 8 am, go to the cafeteria, buy two cups of coffee and two cake doughnuts, and take them up to the branch chief's office. She would go in about 8:15, close the door, and the two of them would stay in there for fifteen minutes or so, doing whatever they were doing, possibly only talking.

The female analyst was quite good and won a coveted overseas assignment for a year. On her last day in the office before she was due to depart, she followed her normal routine at the same time, bought two cups of coffee and two cake doughnuts, and went into the branch chief's office with them, closing the door behind her. That's when her branch mates set in motion their little practical joke. They had gotten a very good looking woman from another office to do the same thing. She came in about 8:20 carrying two cups of coffee and two cake doughnuts, opened the door to the branch chief's office, and walked in.

Stopping then and looking slightly perplexed, she addressed the branch chief saying, "Oh! Did you mean next week?"

The first female analyst jumped up and stormed out of the office, followed by gales of laughter from everyone else who had gathered near the door. The branch chief was furious!

Danger: Fragile

We had obtained a large amount of Waterford crystal that was to serve as a gift for our local liaison colleagues. I asked my friend if the box it came in was adequately bubble-wrapped. Assured by him that it was, I dropped it on the floor, which evoked a loud tinkling sound from inside the box. The wide-eyed foil didn't know that I had swapped the box with one filled with pre-broken glass.

Car Talk

Where would a Washington federal government agency be

without a discussion of parking problems? Be careful who knows where you park. A DI financial analyst bragged about the fantastic mileage that he was getting from his new Geo Metro. "Seventy mpg! Honest!" What he didn't know was that his officemates were bringing in gas cans and fillin' 'er up in the parking lot. (A variant of this was reported in the 1930s by humorist H. Allen Smith in his classic work on practical jokes in which the pranksters, after getting their foil used to seventy mpg, broke his spirit by siphoning the gas from his tank every day, giving him three mpg. The prank was pulled in the 1950s by DI analysts who could take no more bragging by a colleague who had just returned from a TDY in Germany where he had purchased a newfangled VW bug.) The pranksters also toyed with an individual who was on a diet, getting access to his tool belt and changing its size back and forth, so that he thought he was seesawing between major weight gains and losses.

A similar prank was pulled in the 1950s on a dapper fellow who was enamored of his Borsalino hat. The immaculate dresser in the DI's shipbuilding branch proudly showed his Italian, $30 (in a time when a standard Adams hat cost $5) chapeau to all. His office, um, passed the hat to take up a collection, and bought the hat's twin, but in the largest size possible, and even mimicked the initials the foil had stitched on the inside. When he wasn't looking, they switched the hats. He put on the hat, which promptly fell over his ears. Puzzled, he examined the hat, the stitching, and, convinced that it was the real McCoy, scratched his head to see if anything had occurred upstairs to cause this sudden change.

A DI analyst was proud of his new VW Karmann Ghia, but not so proud of the record keeping of his car company's credit service, which often lost his checks. He'd spend hours every month arguing with them over the phone that their dunning letters were inappropriate. One day, several of his burly officemates went out to the parking lot and lifted the car to another location some distance away. His secretary notified him that the Visitor Control Center had called to ask to let in the repo team. Not knowing what else to do, she had approved their entrance. He ran out to his parking space, only to discover that the beloved car was missing. Crestfallen, he returned to his office, where he had a lengthy and spirited discussion with a befuddled credit service representative until his colleagues let him in on the gag.

Don't leave your keys unattended, or you'll find them frozen at the bottom of a cup of water in the office freezer. Same with wet socks hung out to dry, or your wallet (and for good measure, his colleagues canceled the credit cards they found in his wallet).

Overlooked Oversight

Although any federal agency's relationship with its oversight committees will be strained at times, humor often defuses the tension.

The Director of Congressional Affairs (OCA) for the Agency once called from his office to one of his charges, disguising his voice as a well-known Congressional staffer and reading the riot act to the OCA officer. Seven months later, it was time for payback. The Agency officer arranged with Rep. Benjamin Gilman, who was on the Oversight committee, to call the OCA Director during a party to read *him* the riot act. A series of "yessir," "of course, sir," "right away, sir" ensued before it dawned on him that he'd been had. (A similar prank was pulled following the tenure of DCI Judge William Webster, whose ex-staffers had thoughtfully brought him his tax returns to his Washington office. The courier then called the folks back home, falsely warning that the Judge was miffed that one of the forms was missing and that according to his calculations, there appeared to be hell to pay on several counts.)

After a long and tortuous Congressional Budget Justification process, the Office of Congressional Affairs challenged its hallway neighbors, the Chief Financial Officer's staff, to a hallway bowling tournament, using their long, shared corridor and large potato chip plastic canisters as pins. The teams made up team shirts, an overhead projector kept score, a medicine ball and giant exercise ball from the gym were used for those particularly difficult 7-10 splits, and memorial photos were taken. (Editor's note: Alas, several of the worthies remain under cover, so the photo lies on the cutting room floor.)

OCA staffers did their best to clean up their offices for Family Day, when Agency officers bring in their close family members to see the Agency and the office spaces. One staffer, proudly opening his door, was showered with confetti from the shredders, and found mountains of beer cans, soda cans, and other detritus decorating his until-recently-pristine office. As payback, he put forty pounds of rice in their desk drawers, and emptied hole punches inside their umbrellas, which showered them when they opened their umbrellas when going home during the next rainstorm.

A similar Family Day prank was pulled on a rookie attorney with the Office of General Counsel. He was proud of his first office, and brought his wife and kids to show them the place. When he opened his door, a colleague was sitting in his chair and all of his stuff had been moved to a nearby broom closet.

After an especially tense Working Capital Fund meeting, a senior officer brought in Oriental Trading Company spring-loaded jumping frogs. He passed them around at the next staff meeting, had everyone set up several of them in front of their spaces on the table, then conducted a meeting to the entertainment of the staff, wondering whose ticking time bombs would go off first.

In testifying before the President's Foreign Intelligence Advisory Board regarding the planning for the proposed Manned Orbiting Lab, an Air Force project, a senior analyst was pressed about whether he could confirm that we had four-inch resolution on our overhead reconnaissance, given that we were using normal film. He explained that we had overhead of a communist soldier, relieving himself, and he seemed to be well endowed. Case closed.

Words To Live By

My boss eventually accepted that my practical joking was part of the cost of having me on his team, and just gave me three rules of engagement:

—Don't be cruel.

—Don't do anything I have to hear about.

—Don't destroy government equipment.

Sounds like a workable code of ethics for pranksters, and for life in general.

Fun with Phones

Bart Simpson harassed Moe Sislak for years with his prank phone calls asking for Prince Albert in a Can, et al. Agency variants rely on ubiquitous phone message notes. An early variant of Bart's joke asked the foil to "call Mr. Lyons," whereupon he dials the number and gets the zoo. Here are a few more:

In the Original Headquarters Building, each of the elevator cores had telephones in the elevator cars. Rather than connecting to the Security Protective Officer desk or a Facilities duty office when the receiver was lifted, these telephones enabled a person to call any nonsecure extension within Headquarters. These phones could also receive calls from any nonsecure extension in Headquarters. Armed with this knowledge, the prankster obtained the number from one of the elevator phones. Knowing that the target of the prank is away from the office, the prankster calls the foil's secretary, leaving a message to call "Mr. G. Owen Downs." He leaves the phone number from the elevator as the number to return the call. The prankster instructs the secretary that the best time to call is before 8:30 am and after 4 pm—the time of heaviest elevator traffic. Upon finding the telephone call note, the foil calls the number, asks for Mr. Downs, and is told that he has reached an elevator.

Another phone/elevator prank involved a bit of advance

planning. Party A and Party B are in league with each other. At the end of the workday, Party B remains behind in the office for about five minutes, while Party A proceeds to the elevator. While Party A is on the elevator, hopefully crowded with other people also leaving at the end of the workday, Party B dials the telephone number of that elevator core. Party A, in full view of the other passengers, answers the phone, says "I told you not to call me here!" and hangs up, leaving the other passengers flabbergasted.

Someone had obtained a station's outside phone number and was frequently calling, demanding that the CIA stop sexually harassing him via his computer. He even identified himself. The FBI was called and the man was hauled in. He had a mental illness. He would not have obtained the help he needed if he hadn't called the right place.

When the individual, secure lines on each desk were introduced and the ability to "call forward" was generally available, the evening of March 31, two individuals in an office went around and forwarded *every* line to the Front Office secretary's desk. Next morning, April 1, her phone rang every nine seconds. The only way to stop it was for her to go around and "cancel" every phone in the office.

A variation on this gag is a call-forward chain, in which the phone system can be put on an infinite loop of answering machines.

One officemate uttered an especially loud "hello" when answering his phone, to the irritation of the rest of the cubicle farm. Unfortunately for him, he was up against several masters of the practical joke, who reprogrammed his home answering machine to forward to his office phone. Upon picking up his ringing phone, the bewildered recipient would hear his own voice asking him to leave a message. When the novelty wore off, the miscreants taped the phone's receiver plugs down, so that the phone would keep ringing even when he answered it. Pulling the tape off brought him no respite; they had removed the mouthpiece's internal electronics. He thought he'd foiled his tormentors after finding all of these minor traps, but he was amazed to discover that his phone was still ringing and ignoring his "hello." Our heroes had placed a dummy phone—found in the hallways—on his desk, and taped the real phone underneath his desk. His wife refused to believe his protestations that he *was* in, just unable to answer her.

The nightmare wasn't over for him, however. A local pizza delivery service distributed thousands of fliers with one major typo—his, rather than their, phone number.

Not to be outdone, at the National Security Agency, "before we hired too many lawyers, we would wait for a new employee to start talking about a phone conversation they'd had with a girl friend, their mother, their proctologist—you name it—and in some subtle form or another, we would 'give away' the idea that the information was *not news* to the listener. In the hands of a master, this could quickly induce all sorts of paranoia that the agency was tapping the phones of its employees."

When I was escorting members of the news media, I'd say that my cell phone had just started vibrating and I had to take the call. All they would hear from my side was, "Jimmy caught bin Laden?! That's great!" and see how long it would take the reporters to rush to their phones to be the first to report this scoop.

On April 1, 1994, I received a phone message slip on my desk to call "Bob." I called the number and got into a lengthy discussion with whom I soon discovered was Director Robert Gates's secretary. I was quite embarrassed. Two hours later, the person who had slipped me this little note received an extremely well counterfeited "salary overpayment" letter from Payroll. It told him that he had been overpaid to the tune of $2,400, and that $800 would be deducted from each of his next three paychecks. It took him an anxious twenty minutes to find out he'd been had.

I don't believe in coincidence. Returning from a bomb detection seminar, I discovered a tableau on my desk that resembled a bomb. I soon learned that it was testing equipment left by the phone recapitalization folks, but I still don't trust my phone (and some day, I've *got* to get an unlisted secure line!)

I had arranged to call a developmental—a not-yet-recruited asset—at his office, but his secretary intercepted incoming phone calls. I told him "this is Mr. Kim calling for Mr. Chung." The secretary dutifully, if incorrectly, put me through to Mr. Kim's office. After an Abbott and Costello-like exchange of "I'm Mr. Kim," "No, I'm Mr. Kim," I discovered that the other Mr. Kim happened to be on our list of individuals we had hoped to contact. So I took advantage of the situation and invited him out to lunch. Once a case officer, always a case officer, and I managed to recruit him! He became one of our most productive sources. And all because of a misrouted phone call.

Fun With Film

One night, when I was analyzing imagery just taken, I was startled to a full adrenaline rush when I observed something that looked like every description that I had ever seen or heard of a flying saucer! I rubbed my eyes for a full two minutes before looking back into the microscope and, sure enough, it was still there—no delusions! I sheepishly called my supervisor over to the light table and was fully prepared for laughter and abuse once I told him what I was seeing. Once he looked, others came to see, and we began to talk about what our morning report would sound like to the outside world. We called in the imagery scientists who supported the imagery analysts in our facility and they took down the information about the frame of imagery and scurried off to examine the collection parameters. After several hours they came back to me with two images on an 8 x 11 print—one of the "flying saucer" and one that was orthorectified to account for the difference in focus from the satellite's camera. In the rectified image, my flying saucer had become a weather balloon. The effect of a high-flying object imaged by a camera that was focusing on the earth's surface had shortened the balloon into the saucer shape— at least that was the story they were telling me! After some good laughter it was decided that we would do a "flying saucer" briefing for the group chief in the am, and then destroy the briefing so that there was no chance of the *Washington Post* front page. But I still think it was a flying saucer.

A Funny Thing Happened on the Way to the Ops Meeting

In training, you get to make your mistakes in a friendly environment and learn from them. Making the same mistakes "in the wild" can get your assets killed. Here are a few things that happened in my training class:

We were learning how to be a surveillance team, but we also learned something about the difference in perceptions between men and women. Armed with a batch of radios and chase cars, one group of female rookie ops officers and a separate group of male rookie ops officers followed the "rabbits" on a main road. The chase cars were to describe the rabbit car to the next teams, which had yet to be spotted by the alert rabbits. The male team described the car as a stock 1981 Toyota Corona LX sedan. The women's team described the same vehicle as a "teal" car. The descriptions, although radically different, worked.

The same teams followed the rabbits to a local burger emporium, parking within sight of the parking lot. They watched as the couple got take-out orders, but then sat in their cars. The men's team immediately radioed Control, apoplectic that the rabbits were trying to catch their surveillance teams by sitting and watching for cars that were loitering in the area too long. The women's team, noting that the rabbits were women, explained that the rabbits were simply eating their fries before they got cold, something that would not occur to a cold-fries-eating male contingent. Thank God for diversity.

When I got to be on foot surveillance, I was paired with a very attractive, flashy blond as her ostensible husband out for a walk on the town. At the end of the exercise, the rabbits had spotted her, but were not even aware that a guy was with her. I credit her beauty rather than my skills for my blending into the background.

Or perhaps she was "made" by the rabbits during a handoff from one radio team to the other. She ran into the women's restroom to get her radio gear. Wanting to make sure that everything worked, she radioed "Hello, Control. This is surveillant One, over." Alas, the female rabbit was in the next stall.

You get to do more than just be surveillance and spot surveillance in training. You also have to pick places to meet agents, or at least leave messages for them. Picking the right place for the right agent is crucial. One trainee carefully surveilled a location to make sure that it had no police or others likely to break in to the meeting at a sensitive time. Unfortunately, the men's restroom wasn't precisely the right location for the female agent, known to the trainee only as "Pat." Another one of our trainees dutifully showed up on time to a location he had carefully surveilled several times, only to discover that the local Department of Public Works had condemned the building and was in the process of tearing it down, all behind police tape. Allen Dulles told a similar story, in which a dead drop was buried by the Highway Department beneath a mountain of dirt between the time the case officer had made the emplacement and later in the day when the asset was to retrieve it.

All of one's training culminates in final tests, which are usually "live" exercises rather than paper-and-pencil tests (I'll explain to you Millennial Generation members what paper and pencils were a bit later). But to keep the trainees on their toes, this fake test made the rounds among the rookies:

1. You are having lunch with a prospective Agent. During the conversation, a blonde walks into the restaurant and is so stunning, you draw your companion's attention to her and give a vivid description of what you would do if you had her in bed. She walks over to your table and introduces herself as your companion's daughter. Your next move is to:
   a. Ask for her hand in marriage.
   b. Pretend you've forgotten how to speak Spanish.
   c. Repeat the conversation to the daughter and just hope for the best.

2. You are making a presentation to the Ambassador and his staff. The hot enchilada casserole and egg salad sandwich you had for lunch reacts, creating a severe pressure. Your sphincter loses control and you break wind, causing three water tumblers to shatter and a secretary to faint. You should:
   a. Offer to come back next week when the smell has gone away.
   b. Point to the Ambassador and accuse him of the act.
   c. Challenge anyone in the room to do better.

3. You are at the Ambassador's house for lunch when you are suddenly overcome with an uncontrollable desire to pick your nose. You should:
   a. Pretend to wave to someone across the room and with one fluid motion, bury your forefinger in your nostril right up to the fourth joint.
   b. Get everyone drunk and organize a nose picking contest with a prize to anyone who makes their nose bleed first.
   c. Drop your napkin on the floor and when you bend over to pick it up, blow your nose on your sock.

4. You've spent the entire evening with an agent who invited you to an all-night boiler-maker drinking party. You arrive home just

in time to go to work. You stagger to the men's room and spend the next half hour vomiting. As you are washing up at the sink, the Chief of Station (COS) walks up, blows his cigar smoke in your face, and asks you to join him for drinks after work. You:

  a. Look him straight in the eye and launch one last convulsion at the front of his Hart, Shaffner & Marx suit.
  b. Nail him right in the crotch, hoping he will never recognize your green face.
  c. Grasp his hand and pump it until he pees in his pants.

5. You are on your way to meet an agent when your zipper breaks and you discover you forgot to put your underpants on that morning. You decide to:

  a. Call on the Agent's wife instead.
  b. Explain you were just trolling for (write your own joke here).
  c. Purchase a baggy raincoat and head for the nearest (write your own joke here).

6. You have just returned from a short vacation in Green Bay, Wisconsin in January. While briefing your Division Chief, you mention the vacation, and tell him that only whores and football players live there. He responds that his wife is from Green Bay. You:

  a. Ask what position she played.
  b. Ask if she is still working the streets.
  c. Pretend you are suffering from amnesia and do not remember your name.

7. You are having dinner out with an agent and his wife. She looks like she was beaten over the head with an ugly stick and reminds you of the regional runner up of a female-impersonator lookalike contest. Half way through dinner, you feel a hand on your lap. Being resourceful, you:

  a. Accidentally spill hot coffee in your lap.

b. Slip a note to the waiter to have the agent paged and see if the hand goes away when he does.

c. Excuse yourself to go to the men's room. If he follows, do not come out until your shorts rot.

That one was just a midterm, warming up the rookies for their real examination. For this exam, they were expected to converse fluently in a number of fields when dealing with potential agents from diverse backgrounds:

Instructions: Read each question carefully. Answer all questions. You have four hours.

1. History: Describe the history of the Papacy from its origins to the present day, concentrating especially, but not exclusively, on its social, political, economic, religious, and philosophical impact on Europe, Asia, America, and Africa. Be brief, concise, and specific.

2. Medicine: You have been provided with a razor blade, a piece of gauze, and a bottle of Scotch. Remove your appendix. Do not suture until your work has been inspected. You have fifteen minutes.

3. Public Speaking: 2,500 riot-crazed aborigines are storming the classroom. Calm them. You may use any ancient language except Latin and Greek.

4. Biology: Create life. Estimate the differences in subsequent human culture if this form of life had developed 500 million years earlier, with special attention to its probable effect on the English Parliamentary system. Prove your thesis.

5. Music: Write a piano concerto. Orchestrate and perform it with flute and drum. You will find a piano under your seat.

6. Psychology: Based on your knowledge of their works, evaluate the emotional stability, degree of adjustment, and resultant frustrations of each of the following: Alexander of Aphrodesia, Ramses II, Gregory of Nicea, and Hammurabi. Support your evaluation with quotations from each man's work, making appropriate references. It is not necessary to translate.

7. Sociology: Estimate the sociological problems which might accompany the end of the world. Construct an experiment to test your theory.

8. Management Science: Define management. Define science. How do they relate? Why? Create a generalized algorithm to optimize all managerial decisions. Assuming an 1130 CPU supporting fifty terminals, with each terminal to activate your algorithm, design the communications interface and all necessary control programs.

9. Engineering: The disassembled parts of a high-powered rifle have been placed in a box on your desk. You will also find an instruction manual printed in Kiswahili. In ten minutes a hungry Bengal tiger will be admitted to the room. Take whatever action you feel is appropriate. Be prepared to justify your decision.

10. Economics: Develop a realistic plan for refinancing the national debt. Trace the possible effects of your plan in the following areas: Cubism, the Donatist controversy, and the wave theory of light. Outline a method for preventing these effects. Criticize this method from all possible points of view. Point out the deficiencies in your point of view as demonstrated in your answer to the last question.

11. Political Science: There is a red telephone on the desk beside you. Start World War III. Report at length on its socio-political effects, if any.

12. Epistemology: Take a position for or against truth. Prove the validity of your position.

13. Philosophy: Sketch the development of human thought. Estimate its significance. Compare with the development of any other kind of thought.

14. General knowledge: Describe in detail. Be objective and specific.

15. Extra credit: Define the universe. Give three examples.

A spoof program of summer courses available from CIA University (CIAU) also made the rounds:

Self-improvement Workshops
Creative Suffering
Overcoming Peace of Mind
You and Your Birthmark
Guilt without Sex
The Primal Shrug
Holding Your Child's Attention Through Guilt and Fear
Dealing with Post Self-Realization Depression
Whine Your Way to Alienation
How to Overcome Self-Doubt Through Pretense and Ostentation

Business/Career Workshops
Money Can Make You Rich

Talking Good: How You Can Improve Speech and Get a Better Job
I Made $200 in Real Estate
Career Opportunities in North Korea
Under-Achievers Guide to Very Small Business Opportunities
Filler Phrases for Thesis Writers
Tax Shelters for the Indigent
Home Economics Workshops
How You Can Convert Your Family Room Into a Garage
How to Cultivate Viruses in Your Refrigerator
Burglar-Proof Your Home with Concrete
Basic Kitchen Taxidermy
Sinus Drainage at Home

101 Other Uses for Your Vacuum Cleaner

How to Convert a Wheelchair into a Dune Buggy

What To Do With Your Conversation Pit

Health and Fitness Workshops

Creative Tooth Decay

The Joys of Hypochondria

High Fiber Sex

Suicide and Your Health

Bio-feedback and How to Stop It

Skate Your Way to Regularity

Tap Dance Your Way to Social Ridicule

Optional Body Functions

Crafts Workshops

Self-Actualization Through Macrame

Cuticle Crafts

Bonsai Your Pet

Language training is also a key part of an officer's preparation for overseas work. During a particularly tense time in the Middle East, the following list was passed around:

Useful Phrases To Know When Traveling in Terrorist Areas

1. *Akbar khali-kili haftir lotfan.*
   Thank you for showing me your marvelous gun.
2. *Fekr gabul cardan davit paeh gush divar.*
   I am delighted to accept your kind invitation to lie down on the floor with my arms above my head and my legs apart.
3. *Shomaeh fekr tamomeh qeh gofteh bandeh.*
   I agree with everything you have ever said or thought in your life.
4. *Auto arraregh davateman mano sepaheh-hast.*
   It is exceptionally kind of you to allow me to travel in the trunk of your car.
5. *Fashal-eh tupehman na degat mano goftam cheeshayeh mohema rajebeh keshvarehman.*
   If you will do me the kindness of not harming my appendages, I will gladly reciprocate by betraying my country in public.

6.   *Khrel, jepaheh maneh va jayeh amerikahey.*
   I will tell you the names and addresses of many American spies traveling as reporters.
7.   *Balli, balli, balli!*
   Whatever you say.
8.   *Maternier ghermez ahlieh, ghorban.*
   The red blindfold would be lovely, excellency.
9.   *Tikeh nuneh ba ob khreleh bezorg va khrube boyast ino begeram.*
   The water-soaked bread crumbs are delicious, thank you. I must have the recipe.
10.   *Ethehfor'an, ehratee, otageh shoma mikrastam khe do haftaeh ba bodaneh Sheereel Teegz.*
   Truly, I would rather be a hostage to your greatly esteemed self than spend a fortnight upon the person of Cheryl Tiegs.

Lost in Translation

When serving overseas, we're often summoned to formal dinner affairs, which require the hosts and guests to toast each other in increasing measures of grandiloquence. Summoning up my best knowledge of the local language, I thought I was saying "I want to salute our joint endeavors," but the crowd heard me say "I want to vomit." Maybe I was accurate . . .

Allen Dulles told the story of the chutzpah of one of his assets during WWII, the Zurich representative of Admiral Canaris, head of German military intelligence. Two members of the German legation spotted the agent meeting with Dulles and confronted him, accusing him of working with Dulles and the OSS. The asset went on the attack, saying that of course he was meeting Dulles, who was his chief source on Allied affairs. He warned that if they told anyone about this source, he would ensure that they would never work in the German diplomatic corps again. He added that the Dulles contact was ultra-secret, known only to Admiral Canaris and the senior-most levels of the German government. They apologized, and shuffled off. The asset was not exposed.

Travel for operations also has complications, particularly in the Middle East, as shown by these three stories:

In departing from his European location, an officer we'll call Joe was consigned to a Middle Eastern airline service. Before boarding, travelers have to go on the tarmac to identify personal luggage so they can be loaded on the aircraft. Upon taking off Joe looked out the window and saw all the luggage was still on the tarmac. When checking for his luggage at his Middle Eastern duty station, he was advised it would be placed on a later flight and delivered to his hotel room. Not being a seasoned traveler, Joe failed to take a carryon bag with essentials, i.e. a change of underwear and toiletries. To add to this nightmare, Joe was assigned a room on the twelfth floor, just below the all night bar and belly dancer entertainment. Things couldn't get any worse for Joe, right? Wrong. During his first day at work he was moving equipment around and split his only pair of pants in the seat. The station communicator used a hand stapler to fix his pants. Fortunately, Joe's personal luggage showed up that afternoon. Incidentally, Joe also had the hotel relocate him to a lower floor.

On Joe's trip to another country, he went to meet with his contact regarding equipment disposal. The local security personnel would not let him in because he looked suspect, i.e. Joe was wearing sunglasses and had a small mustache, typical of a terrorist profile. Joe showed them his passport and they still refused to let him enter the compound. Joe had to go back to his hotel room and call his contact and arrange for a meeting at the main entrance. Upon returning to Europe, Joe shaved his mustache and quit wearing sunglasses.

When Joe was traveling to yet another country, he decided to visit a historical site. During the tour a group of ladies from the US approached him and asked him very slowly, using hand signals, for the local time. Upon responding with the time, the ladies were amazed at his excellent English and complimented him. Joe's response was to tell them that he should be able to speak excellent English—he's from New Jersey.

The Middle East isn't the only tough place to travel. My best friend reported from his first posting in Africa:

When we arrived a couple of weeks ago (at 2 am, three hours late, and with all of our baggage lost somewhere in Lagos Airport), we noticed a rather odd smell in the baggage claim area. Ignoring it at first, we started to feel a bit nauseous because of its overwhelming smell. After looking around, we noticed a cardboard box ripped open on the side, and—hold on to your socks—a pig's head hanging out of it. Closer examination revealed that someone had shipped, in their baggage, a dead pig wrapped in variety of vegetables and grasses. Not only that but it wasn't dressed or cut up. When the obvious local came to pick it up and dragged it away, blood started pouring out of the back of the box. Such is life in West Africa.

During my friend's first overseas tour, we'd arranged that three of us would meet at a local watering hole for an ops meeting after we'd conducted separate surveillance detection runs to ensure that we were surveillance-free. The two veterans showed up at the site on time, clean, wondering where our rookie was. Time passed. More time passed. After half an hour, we spotted him running down the street toward us, yelling "My car's on fire." Not the best way to lull surveillance via non-alerting behavior.

Sometimes in espionage, there are no hard feelings. Vivacious Valentina, a suspected KGB informer, ran the barbershop and beauty salon in the US Embassy's basement. Although she was eventually found out and fired, she was still treated to a going-away party by her American customers.

The KGB's portable x-ray device, which safecrackers usually held in their teeth, thereby freeing their hands, allowed them to watch tumblers moving into place. However, the device emitted high levels of radiation. KGB safecrackers were called *bezzubyye,* "the guys with no teeth."

The Agency's audio techs also had on-the-job difficulties. One particularly parsimonious tech was in charge of provisions for a team that was in close quarters for several days. He bought beer— because it was safer than the water—and canned tuna, period. After several days of unbearable heat and world-class bad breath, the rest of the team voted that he would never again have food acquisition duties.

As was the motto of the Office of Public Affairs, "it could have been worse." It was worse for one tech in Africa. To get onto a targeted compound somewhere in Africa, he jumped over a wall and landed in a benji ditch, filled with "night soil" (raw sewage). After notifying Headquarters, they cabled back, saying "We forgot to tell you. One of the side effects of the African air is a problem with one's sense of balance, causing one to fall into a benji ditch."

My daughter has a unique first name, and when I was meeting in alias with various Martians, it wouldn't do for them to hear her name, trace it through school records, and find out her last name. Because it's rare for Americans to give their child a different last name from either of the parents (Okay, can you name someone besides Tom Hayden and Jane Fonda who did so?), they would quickly determine that the name I'd give them was an alias and that perhaps I was something other than what I'd claimed to be. So we gave her an alias, which would be our own special secret, to be used only when we saw Uncle Vasily. She learned this lesson well. Years later, when she'd go to summer schools and the students were introducing themselves around, she'd throw out an alias, which she kept for the entire summer. We learned about her habit when we had a parent-teacher conference and asked how Sally was doing. "But I have no Sally in my class." Looking out the window, we pointed out our daughter chatting with her classmates. "Oh, but her name's Jill!" My daughter. She'll be a great case officer some day.

I had just come home from an overseas ops meeting when I was greeted by my wife and a neighbor exiting our house. My wife gave me an unusually passionate kiss in front of the neighbor, giving her time to whisper to me, "Your asset is stashed in the upstairs den!" before breaking the embrace. She shepherded the neighbor over to her house while I sidled up the stairs to discover one of my assets, snoozing comfortably on my office couch.

I was assigned to conduct a countersurveillance operation for a colleague overseas. I asked my wife to accompany me. She was perfect cover: the local service would never believe that an 8½-month pregnant woman would be conducting a countersurveillance run!

When he was Chief of Station in El Salvador, Dave Phillips, author of *Nightwatch,* was asked to ensure that the newly-restored democratically elected president stayed in seat. The major threat against the president's tenure, and that of the democratic system, was the previous general who had run the country and decided to stay, acting as a breathing Sword of Damocles. Over a series of meetings, COS Phillips managed to persuade the general to leave the country for a very cushy lifestyle in Miami, courtesy of Uncle Sam. But there was one hitch—he wanted some sort of signal by the U.S. Ambassador that this wasn't just a CIA ploy: that the U.S. Department of State was on board with this plan. Phillips suggested that when the general next saw the Ambassador, if that worthy tugged on his right earlobe *a la* Carol Burnett, it was a signal that the USG was supportive. Phillips's work wasn't over, however. He had to approach a very senior, patrician, socially conservative, career diplomat in Ambassador Ellsworth Bunker. Phillips plunged into the fray, and sounded out Ambassador Bunker, who responded, "Mr. Phillips, you have a deal. I would piss in a potted plant if it meant that you could get the general out of town!"

A walk-in is someone who comes to an official installation unannounced, usually after hours, to ask for assistance. He may want to apply for asylum, to seek a handout, or to report something he believes may be of interest to the USG. Most of these walk-ins are of limited value to us. Many are just plain coo-coo or are con men of one sort or another. On occasion, however, the walk-in may be someone about whom we want to learn more. Separating the wheat from the chaff is a tedious task but one that must be conducted professionally and securely.

The Marine Guards protecting U.S. Government installations are usually the first contact the walk-in has with U.S. officials. Therefore, the stations pay special attention to training the Guards on how to handle the walk-ins in a secure and efficient manner. But, it doesn't always work that way. In one instance, the Guard's instruction was to let the walk-in into the installation and hold him in a secure area. He was then to telephone the station's duty officer to ask him/her to come to the embassy (thus, starting the process to determine whether the walk-in might be one of the good ones). The Marine was trained to follow a short, simple script. He was not to elaborate, nor to use names.

In this case, however, an obviously flustered Marine blurted out the name of the officer, saying, "Mr. (Jones), sir, there is a man in the garage and she's hysterical!"

Recognition Signals

Someone called the embassy to offer information on clandestine arms shipments. He was calling from a neighboring county. Meeting arrangements were complicated by the fact that he said that he would be catching a ferry to come to the meeting. (The ferrys did not have a good on-time record, especially during the winter months.) He insisted that we would be able to recognize him, because he would be carrying the current issue of *Time* magazine in his left hand. Although leaving the mechanics of the meeting in his hands was not good tradecraft, he made it take-it-or-leave-it, so we had no choice. We finally agreed that we would meet at 8 pm in front of a newsreel theater at the railroad station near the ferry landing.

At the appointed time, I was there, but he wasn't. Nor was he on the next ferry. Finally, he showed up. But without *Time*. Instead, he was carrying a copy of *Life*. "I couldn't find a copy of *Time*," he said. "But I knew that you would figure it out," he said. "After all, they are published by the same company."

An officer set up a meeting with the recognition signal to be the contact to be carrying the day's edition of the *Financial Times*, explaining that *FT*'s are easy to spot because they are printed on salmon-colored paper. That would have been okay, if the *FT* hadn't been on strike for a couple of weeks!

I was to meet an in-transit TDYer in the transit lounge at the airport. I dictated a cable to confirm the arrangements. Because we did not know each other, I said that I was "fat, bald, and six feet tall." Miss Innocence paused in her typing to comment, "I didn't know you were six feet tall!!"

Sy Goodrich wrote in his memoirs *Born To Spy: Recollections of a CIA Case Officer* that he recruited the wrong French Communist Party official. Sy picked the wrong man from a station mug book, invited him for lunch, realized he had erred, but recruited him anyway.

Our ethnic Chinese agent had done an outstanding job in a recruitment of a local communist. Looking to repeat that success, we found another target and began preparing him for the new operation. He was absolutely impossible—froze up, forgot to ask the right questions, and couldn't even respond to comments about party matters. We discovered that in the first recruitment, he had had to use an interpreter. . . . Our man spoke no Malay and the target spoke no Chinese. The interpreter took our asset's clumsy comments and "translated" them for the target. Our asset could have recited the phone book and the interpreter would have made the conversation sensible. When the branch chief asked why we had done so, we replied that he was all too scrutable.

We supported an anti-Soviet exile group called by its initials. They built up a considerable infrastructure in a particular country, including several storage facilities. Story has it that a local demolition firm was contacted by some men who claimed to be officers of the organization (and had ID to prove it). They contracted with the firm to demolish a warehouse that the organization owned and was standing empty. It wasn't until the firm sent its bill that anyone realized that this was a Russian version of what Casey called "Soft CA," or "soft covert action," of playing with the opposition's head.

Assets often pretend to understand English better than they do. That can lead to problems. One asset I handled spoke quite good colloquial English . . . but with gaps. During a meeting, I went over emergency contact instructions in case we missed a scheduled meeting. On the first Tuesday of each month, go to the city museum at noon and someone will approach you carrying your photo, etc. I asked him to repeat the plan and he did. Then he asked, "'Noon,' that is around two o'clock, isn't it?"

A case officer wanted to wear a disguise to a meeting with a new asset. An OTS makeup wizard made the C/O into another person, including dying his hair red. The C/O went off to the meeting site. It began to rain. Soon, the C/O was drenched. As he was hurrying along, the C/O caught sight of himself in a shop window. The hair dye, when wet, turned from red to green. It was cascading down his face, turning him into a credible imitation of the Incredible Hulk!

After completing an audio installation, a tech (for reasons known only to him), drew a mustache on a poster of Chairman Mao. It did not go unnoticed by the office staff.

Audio installations often require pieces of wood designed to look like other braces on the bottom of a piece of furniture. Someone branded some of these on the side that was glued to the furniture. If discovered, the branding would be easily recognized—it was TOYS ARE US.

British intelligence officer Malcolm Muggeridge wrote in his book *The Infernal Grove: Chronicles of Wasted Time,* that "In coded messages, countries had always to be referred to by symbols—Germany, for instance, was 'Twelve-land.' The practice was scrupulously observed throughout the war even though, on one festive occasion at an Istanbul hotel, when the orchestra played the German national anthem, the staff of the German embassy stood to attention and sang as one man: '*Zwolfte-land, Zwolfte-land, uber alles!*'"

Battles with the Budget and the Budgeteers

When I was in Payroll in the mid-1990s, I was in the section that processed retirements, early outs, judgments, etc. We received a letter from the Internal Revenue Service telling us to dock an employee's salary for Federal back-taxes owed. Once we started, we received a cease and desist letter from the employee stating that he didn't have to pay taxes because Virginia was not part of the United States. The letter went on to advise that Virginia never rejoined the Union after the Civil War; that was why it was the Commonwealth of Virginia—it was its own country. We sent a copy of the letter to the Office of Medical Service, who alerted Security. The only thing we heard afterwards was that the gentleman was being evaluated.

This story might be apocryphal, but it illustrates the occasional tension between the operations officers— spyrunners—in the field and the Budget and Finance professionals. An operations officer arranged to meet a foreign agent on an out-of-the-way street corner. Although our officer arrived on time, the agent did not. Alas, it soon began to rain. The intrepid officer ducked into a nearby haberdashery, bought a rain hat, and ran back out to his asset meeting. Alas, the asset never showed and after an hour, the officer went back to the Station to complete his accounting.

With all of the expenses of mileage, parking, etc., the total came to $50. The B&F shop returned his accounting with a notation "hat denied, please resubmit." The officer redid his accounting, sans hat, but sent in the same $50 total, with an annotation, "Find the Hat!"

Homegrown Humor

In 1990, I took up a new hobby: performing local stand-up comedy. I played in perhaps a half-dozen clubs in Washington, D.C., Virginia, and Maryland. Happily for the industry, I decided to keep my day job. But before I became a recovering standup, I formed the Agency Comedy Club, which gave me a chance to try out material with a friendly audience before taking it on the road. Fellow Agency employees used the club to try out their Toastmasters-worthy humorous speeches.

The tradition of internal Agency comedy has continued, be it in skits at office holiday parties, in photocopier humor described elsewhere in this collection, or in impromptu writing contests. The Agency Writers Group, known to its members as Invisible Ink, recently hosted its equivalent of the Washington Post's Style Invitational, in which contestants were asked to provide the punch line for the opening "Two Spies Walk Into a Bar . . ." Among the entries were:

—I'm sorry, you're not cleared to read the punch line.

—The Defense Intelligence Agency refused to coordinate on the punch line.

—Surveillance lost them at this point, and we can only speculate on what occurred after that.

—Budget and Finance questioned Surveillance's accounting, saying paying for drinks while trying to blend in to the background was nonetheless against regulations.

—The Employee Assistance Program scheduled an intervention. Drinking on the job is unacceptable.

—but their handler ducks.

—and the bar immediately changes into a dry cleaner's.

—and one says to the other, "Sometimes it's nice to come back from the field and see what is new back here. Wow! The Headquarters cafeteria sure has changed!"

—The first spy flags down the bartender and asks for a traditional martini on the rocks. The other one nudges his buddy to tell a joke and suddenly sees a gun pointed in their direction. In a split second, they both take cover as the bullet flies through the air and vaporizes the speared olive in the martini glass. When the coast is clear, the first spy says, "It is amazing—our taking cover and narrowly escaping." "Yup," says the other spy. "And now my martini is shaken perfectly!"

—followed by a priest, a rabbi, and a Baptist minister; George Clooney, George Tenet, and Curious George; and Money, a Zebra, a grasshopper, a pirate with a parrot on his shoulder, the entire New England Patriots' offensive line, an Eyewitness TV-News camera crew, three nuns carrying golf clubs, a man in a tuxedo with a Marilyn Monroe double and a little ten-inch-tall man on his shoulder, followed by Oliver Stone, Will Smith, William Jefferson Clinton, and the bartender yells, "Hold it! Wait a second! What is this, a joke?!"

—Two spies walk into a bar. Open source reporting suggests that two persons reported to be members of an intelligence service by a source of undetermined reliability (Headquarters Comment: Source is not available for re-contact) walked into an establishment that has a history of providing alcoholic beverages in exchange for monetary compensation . . .

—Two spies, one American, one French, walk into a bar and settle into a quiet corner booth. The Frenchman is jazzed about their joint operation and all the cool technologies his side is going to contribute, not to mention the opportunity before him, but his attractive, yet jet-lagged, American counterpart couldn't give a flying fig; she just wants to have a drink and get some sleep. "But *Cherie,* the night is young, so are we, and there is so much to discuss! I have a proposition for you. No, no, let me explain! Let's play a game—how do you say—a guessing game! And we can make it interesting with a small wager, say, 50 euros? I'll ask you a question, and if you can't answer it, you pay me 50 euros. Then you ask me a question, and if I can't answer it, I'll pay you 50 euros. What do you say?" Sensing her reluctance, the suave Frenchman makes a new offer: "I tell you what! If you can't answer my question, you pay me only 5 euros, but I will still pay you 50 euros if I can't answer yours! Very enticing, no?" Our heroine realizes she's trapped, so she accepts his challenge. "*Tres bon, Cherie!* Ladies first! What is the distance, in meters (We French developed the metric system, you know, and it is much more accurate than your English system of feet and yards and inches, *mon Dieu!*), the distance in meters from here to the moon? No using your pocket GPS!" Annoyed, the American pulls her wallet out and hands the cocky Parisian a crisp 5 euro note. "Now it's my turn. What goes up hill on three legs and downhill on four?" Her cocky counterpart suddenly turns pale. He mutters to himself, first in English, then in French. He stares around the room helplessly, searching for some clue to ease his predicament, but there is no hope for him. After several minutes, he taps the sleepy American on the shoulder, and hands her a 50 euro note. "I surrender!" To his stupefied amazement, she puts the bill in her wallet and rises to leave. "Wait! *Un moment, s'il vous plait!* You must tell me, 'What goes up hill on three legs and downhill on four?' I must know!" The wily spy takes out her wallet, hands him a five euro note, and bids him adieu.

Two case officers are sitting together talking. One C/O says to the other, "Wait a minute! You're lying to me." The other C/O says, "Yeah, I know, but hear me out!"

The second Invitational asked for answers to the classic joke question: Why did the case officer cross the road?

—to see if surveillance would follow.

—to ask surveillance how he was doing so far.

—because it's hard to drive straight when you're always looking at your review mirror to see if surveillance is following you.

—to avoid the Budget and Finance officer who was chasing him down for his delinquent accounting.

—to catch a former CIA employee and tell him a recycled a-man-walks-into-a-bar joke, to which the former employee replies, "Hey, wait a second! I'm retired now! I am out of the loop! Was that supposed to be funny? Was that a joke or a code?"

—Why did the analyst cross the road? The analyst, having received information from a reliable source that there is gold in the dirt, assessed that it was time to cash in on pay dirt.

—Why did the analyst cross the road? We can neither confirm nor deny that we have analysts in our employ evaluating the feasibility of crossing roads.

Some jokes are told across the Intelligence Community (IC). Everyone's heard from a member of the public who believes that the height of espionage humor is saying "I could tell you, but then I'd have to kill you." More typical of IC humor is this illustration of how some view the Federal Bureau of Investigation (FBI):

At a competition between canine teams from various IC agencies, the finalists were dogs from the Drug Enforcement Administration (DEA), U.S. Secret Service (USSS), the Central Intelligence Agency, and the FBI. The DEA dog went first, sniffed out a stash of cocaine, and came back to his handler. The Secret Service dog sniffed out explosives hidden in a car, defused the bomb, and came back to his handler. The CIA dog spotted a foreign spy in the act of placing a dead drop, retrieved the classified material, and came back to his handler. The FBI dog humped the Secret Service dog, bit the CIA dog, stole the cocaine, and called a press conference to claim credit for the counterspy, explosives, and narcotics busts.

One of the longest-lasting computer-mediated discussion groups is The Users Group (THUGS), which often holds multi-threaded one-upmanships. Among the most enduring/endearing, are these Computer Programming Laws written in 1988:

Any given program, once run, is obsolete.

Any given program costs more and takes longer.

If a program is useful, it will have to be changed.

If a program is useless, it will have to be documented.

Any given program will expand to fill all available memory.

Program complexity grows until it exceeds the capability of the programmer who must maintain it.

Once it is possible for programmers to write programs in English, it will be found that programmers cannot write in English.

The fatal flaw of every program is always found after the system has been in production for several months (see next rule).

Any program tested without flaw will invariably die a horrible death when placed into production.

The value of a given program is in direct proportion to the weight of its output.

No matter how hard you try, nothing can be made fool proof; fools are just too smart.

Any data, no matter how dubious of origin, once processed on a computer is suddenly transformed into facts of religious quality.

If builders built buildings in the same manner as many programmers wrote code, one woodpecker could bring civilization to an end.

Should we ever feel that computers are getting too powerful, we could always organize them into committees—that should slow them down.

Every program works until you try to run it.

Programs should not be documented. If they are hard to write, they should be hard to read.

If a program is made foolproof, only fools will be able to use it.

Three laws of thermodynamics as they apply to programming:

1. Energy and Matter cannot be created or destroyed.

   Translation: You can't win.

2. Entropy always increases.

   Translation: You can't break even.

3. Everything always has at least a minimum amount of energy.

   Translation: You cannot quit the game.

   Variables won't, constants aren't.

   It's not a bug, it's a feature!

Here is a set of rules an application programmer I knew used to justify his work:

1. My code is always right.

2. Once anyone else touches my code, in any way, it is no longer my code.

3. If anyone finds a problem in my code, they touched it, and it is now their problem (see rule #2). After all, *my* code is always right.

The differences between the CIA's analysts, known as DIers (Directorate of Intelligence) and its operational cadre, known as DOers (Directorate of Operations), is shown in this tale offered by an officer who served in both Directorates:

In the backwaters of the Amazon lived two tribes: the DOERs and the DIERs. They were constantly at war—raids, massacres, bloodletting, etc. (Legend has it that the hatred started over dissemination lists and source protection.) In the spirit of *glasnost* and threatened extinction, the DOERs and DIERs started peace negotiations.

For a time, all was quiet on the Amazon front. Then, during a bilateral discussion with a foreign government, the DIERs received a beautiful gold throne encrusted with precious stones. Even though the gift was the work of a worker-bee DIER, the chief of the DIER tribe took possession of the throne and kept it in his office on the seventh floor (where CIA management resides)—not a bad trick for grass-hut building technology.

Anyhow, the DOERs were extremely jealous. After all, they had supplied the information to support the bilateral, which resulted in the throne gift-giving. So the DOERs mounted an operation. After some months of planting *glasnost*-style articles in DIER publications, the DOERs had lulled their unsuspecting enemy into a false sense of security. They stole into the DIERs' village, pillaging and raping as a front for the real object of their desire—the gold throne. (Rumor has it that the DOERs mined the Amazon crossing, but it is still in a tribal inquiry, and may be the subject of a later joke downstream.)

The DIERs were outraged. They knew from reliable sources that the chief DOER had the throne on the seventh floor of his grass hut. When queried on this fact, the DOER villagers just smugly responded with, "You don't have the need to know!"

The DIERs, however, got the last laugh. The structural integrity of grass huts just was not made for gold thrones. During a meeting, the floors collapsed, and the chief DOER subsequently fell to his death.

Alas, with tragedy came some good. The DOERs and the DIERs now have a peace truce. Of course, the new motto they live by is . . .

(pause)

wait for it . . .
(longer pause)
"People who live in grass huts shouldn't stow thrones."

The Comedy Club

Several Agency officers were standup comics before becoming Agency officers and/or during their time with the Agency. In 1990, they created a lunchtime Comedy Club, allowing them to try out some of their material before taking it on the road. The Club also featured Agency-specific in-jokes that would be used only with internal audiences. Members of the Agency's Toastmasters contingent also used the Club to polish their humorous speeches. Some of the performances were classical standup routines; others were Agency-unique skits. A few texts of the performers' material have survived. Some is dated, but a good contemporary history text should help you along the rough spots. These sacred texts will also explain why we decided to keep our day jobs:

Bush, Clinton, Perot, Quayle. (Pause) You're a tough audience. I use the country's top four political jokes, and you don't laugh.

Any smokers here tonight? They can come in handy. I use them to gauge temperature. Degrees Centigrade = (LIM 0-5) smokers/ overcoats x 2 + yards from building (LIM 20). Windchill in degrees = angle smoker's back arches when protecting match from wind. I like to watch them on really cold days, when the windchill freezes your breath, and the smokers are trying to figure out whether they just took a puff or are just breathing.

Senator Byrd has been trying to get the CIA to move to West Virginia, so I've been taking language and banjo lessons. I just can't get the accent right, so I switched to another foreign language:

womenspeak. Have you noticed that they have a private language? Guys, do you have any idea of the meaning of the words: Taupe? Mauve? Teal? Chartreuse? I'm told that you can get a 2+ on your language test if you know the meaning of words like Commitment, Caring, and We've Got to Talk.

I had an amicable divorce, because we had no children. However, we had collected a large number of friends over the years and got into a ferocious custody battle over the Hendersons. It finally settled that I get them on Tuesdays, Thursdays, and alternate holidays.

My wife gave me this grocery list, which includes feminine pads. She wants Maxi mini, Night Supers, Light, Unscented, Medicated with Tabs, forty Megs RAM, cruise control. Naturally, there are about fifty different types of these things, and none of the distinctions mean anything to me. Ever stand there staring at every single box, trying to figure out what she wants, while everyone is thinking, "Uh, oh, call the perv patrol to Aisle 4"? You can't easily turn to a woman in the aisle next to you and ask about these things. "Excuse me, you look like you understand these things. Is 'mini medicated fresh' the same as 'nighttime super thin'?" Some of these things have wings. Wings! These things can fly!? That's an image that's now burned into my brain! And when you get up to the checkout counter, naturally the price stamp is off. So you have to stand there, hiding behind the beets, while they call over the public address system, "Can I get a price check on . . ."

Which got me to thinking, there are FDS products. How come there aren't any MDS? Imagine my surprise when I logged on to the CIA's mainframe . . . *(Editor's Note: The Message Delivery System was commonly known as MDS.)*

Promotions were announced today. I didn't make it. Apparently I had the same panel as Rodney King. DCI Gates announced that there won't be many promotions, and that we have to find other incentives for coming to work. Four people in my office have decided to have affairs with each other. They also said "employees should be encouraged to develop outside interests." In other words, "get a life!" But it's worse in the UK: Even the British Prime Minister is still a Major. *(Editor's Note: John Major.)* West German Chancellor Genscher resigned after eighteen years time in grade. And in the Kennedy family, Arnold Schwarzeneggar has to retire before Sargent Shriver can make Lieutenant.

The latest Career Training class has a woman who is twenty. Twenty! I have ties older than that that! This is probably her first job, and it's likely that she doesn't have too much experience with guys who routinely wear ties throughout the day. Guys signal things by the way they wear their ties. For example, (flip length of tie over knot) this guy has something to hide. This guy (shorten length to several inches above belt buckle) will probably be a flop in bed. This guy (lengthen tie past belt) thinks he's God's gift to women. This guy (stick tie in pants) is God's gift to himself, so don't bother. And this guy (stick tie inside shirt) moonlights at Safeway.

Everyone's talking about the jury's call on Rodney King. They acquitted the officers because they couldn't see all of the baseball bat swings landing. In baseball, if you get a hit one out of three times, you're a hero. In Los Angeles, you're Not Guilty.

Last night I had one of those "Aha!" experiences which gives your life the perspective you've always been seeking. My high school girlfriend, whom I hadn't seen for twenty years, phoned from out of the blue. During the initial "how ya been's" she announced that shortly after we broke up, she discovered that she was a lesbian. I'll have to be honest with you, the first thing that ran through my mind was "Thank you, God. I've got material for the Comedy Club!" Of course, this news explained quite a lot for me. Like why I was the only virgin in my college's freshman class. Like why she'd get huffy when I looked at other women; apparently, it wasn't jealousy—it was competition! We had the same taste in women! Finding out something like this triggers a guy's worst nightmare: You're walking down the street when a former lover spots you and announces to the world "There he is! *That's* the man who made me a homosexual!" Guys also have to resolve news like this. I immediately turned it into a positive commentary on my manhood, figuring "Well, she had the best, so she gave up on the rest."

She also said that she uses all sorts of "underground" directories of places that are sympathetic to lesbians, such as bars, restaurants, etc. They even had lists of garage mechanics. I'm sorry, I don't care if you tell 'em you're gay or not; when an auto mechanic hands you the bill, he's out to screw you.

Well, let's turn to the news. Despite Senator Byrd's continuing efforts, CIA is not moving to West Virginia. I'm a little put out. I had just bought the banjo franchise for the new CIA Headquarters Building. And I was so proud that I'd finally bought an American car—a pickup truck with a gun rack and a huntin' dawg named Blue.

Also in the news: Bill Clinton has said that he used marijuana but didn't inhale. That's like saying he used alcohol but didn't swallow. I bet he stole that line from Miss America.

Jerry Brown has decided to try to reach out and touch black America. Now if only he could reach out his feet and touch terra firma.

Voters and basketball fans are still trying to figure out how Duke made it to the Final (Solution) Four. *(Editor's note: Former Klan leader David Duke had been in the news that week.)*

Did you notice the names of the people who were on the Clarence Thomas-Anita Hill Hearings? Howell, Arlen, Strom, Orrin. I would've been much more comfortable with someone whose first name was Billy Bob. And perhaps with a Cindy.

I used to be a Yuppie, but I had to give it up. It's not politically correct any more, and they're under fire. Yuppies are apparently the last group in America that it's still PC to make fun of. You can't find Purina Yuppie Chow at Gucci Giant in McLean. So I joined Yup-Anon. They get you into redneck chic, buying BMWs with gun racks, and goin' huntin' with a Shar Pei named Blue. Some Yuppies are now sporting designer tattoos. I ran into a guy that had on his arm "Born to Diversify." And I don't care what he says, that BMW logo on his chest does not mean "Be My Woman!" And I don't think the American Eagle tattoo looks right with a briefcase in one claw and a cell phone in the other. One Yuppie woman even tattooed her prenuptial agreement on her thigh.

My ex-wife was into tattoos. She had my name tattooed on her wrist. I got worried when I saw that it was crossed out and replaced by "Jim." Then I got really annoyed when all of the football team's autographs started appearing. To add insult, it was the Dallas Cowboys rather than the Redskins! She also had a tattoo on her tuchus that said "If you can read this, you're too close." In *braille!?* Of course, we had a mixed marriage: she was a tattooed biker, and I ride a tricycle. Things were getting rocky when she started introducing me as her "first husband." Looks like I'm not getting that promotion to "trophy husband."

I turned forty this year, officially making me an Old Fart. But with this baby face, I still get carded. I was in the drugstore the other day. "This ID yours? . . . Okay, here's your Rogaine." I grew up during the sexual revolution. I was a hostage. I remember thinking the Beatles' "I Wanna Hold Your Hand" was about what I could shoot for. But the current number one hit on the radio is "I Touch Myself." While I was in the drugstore, I tried to buy some condoms, but they wouldn't let me. Seems that they now have a 7-day cooling off period . . .

I especially know that I've turned forty in bed. Don't believe those professional athletes; the knees are *not* the first thing to go. When you're reading "How to Drive Your Woman Wild in Bed," she's reading "Method Acting, Chapter Seven: Faking It." You know you're really getting old when you fake it and you're alone.

Now that preschool has started, we're on the hook for coming up with Show and Tell items. We have five years to go, and already we're running out of material—a problem not unique to comics. But my child's a Yuppie: she brings in pasta machines, convertible securities, BMW keys. . . .

Let's see what's in the news. It's scandal season in Washington. We've had Watergates, Irangates, and now: Bob Gates. Who knew? The Special Prosecutor says that where there's smoke, there's Fiers. *(Editor's note: Alan Fiers was a senior Agency official often mentioned in investigations.)*

Princess Di and Prince Charles are having marital difficulties. It could be because of his hobby: he collects antique toilet seats. Does this guy know how to woo women? "So, baby, want to come up to the palace and see my loos?"

I got a haircut this morning. The only reason that I know this is that today twenty-two people told me that I'd gotten a haircut. Why do people need to say "You got a haircut"? I knew what I was getting into when I walked into the barbershop. I didn't just fall asleep, wake up, and notice that someone had stolen part of my hair. And why don't people say whether they like it? It's just that nondescriptive, noncommittal "You got a haircut." Why can't they tell you what they think: "Fraternity initiation, right?" "I warned you about going to trainees in Barber College." "Was the barber coming down from bad 'ludes?"

I have a metric clock. Now I really don't have enough hours in the day. I got only three hours of sleep last night. But at least I work only three hours a day. And I don't have to attend 11 o'clock meetings anymore. My boss called me up to say, "Hey, where are you? It's 11 o'clock." I looked at my clock, said, "No, it's not," and the phone went dead.

We had a pretty good Christmas. My daughter got this young

standup-comic's microphone set. Now she can say "Take my dolly, please." We also got this Night Clock that projects the time on the ceiling. I was embarrassed that I'm this lazy, so I bought a Nordic Track. This thing is supposed to exercise every muscle group at once and is supposed to be good for you. What it means is that every muscle is yelling "Hey, brain, stop this" but each group drowns the others out, the brain can't hear, and you keep exercising.

My wife took me to her office's Christmas party. I didn't know anyone there, so on the drive over, I got the briefing. This is where I learned all of the things I can't say to everyone who's here. Well, it is like trying to obey the order "Okay, now don't think of elephants." So I'm being introduced around:

"Say, from Susan's description, you must be Jill. I wouldn't say you're morbidly obese!"

"Frank, what's that you're drinking? Oh, you're the AA one!"

"Bernie! Glad to see you got off that morals charge!"

For those of you who dread opening that gift from your mother-in-law, just remember my Christmas motto: paranoids are never surprised.

Let's turn to the news. I keep seeing these DUKE bumper stickers. I can't tell if the driver is a Nazi or just likes basketball. *(Editor's note: Again, see David Duke.)*

I see Moscow opened up its first sex shop. You thought the bread line was long! And you were wondering how we were going to keep those Soviet nuclear scientists at home. Brain drain won't be the problem.

Pollsters asked the Presidential candidates what their favorite movies were. David Duke said *Thelma and Louise.* He apparently thought it was *Selma and Louise.* His second choice was *White Christmas.*

We decided to get a nanny for our 3-year-old daughter. We had in mind Mary Poppins. Well, she has an unlisted number. We found out that "nanny" actually means "anything goes." You're never sure what's going to happen during the interview:

"Your application indicates you engage in ritual sacrifice only on major Satanic holy days. Thank you. Next."

"So you want off all American, Christian, Jewish, Muslim, Buddhist, and New Age holidays? Which leaves you available on July 29 in Leap Years. Thank you. Next."

"Your list of references says that you cooked for a doctor. Do you have a phone number for this Dr. Hannibal Lecter? I see. Thank you. Next."

"Your application says that you need to leave early on Fridays so that you can fly to Miami to meet small unmarked planes from Colombia. Thank you. Next."

"You say you're willing to clean. You cleaned out the last house you worked at so well that the police are still looking for you. Thank you. Next."

Dating is getting tougher. Women are demanding cleverer, or at least more sensitive, opening lines. I've been talking to a lot of single women, and they offered the following Top Ten Worst Pickup Lines that they've actually heard:

10. I'd like to drink your bath water.
9. If I could rewrite the alphabet, I'd put U and I together.
8. Let's have breakfast tomorrow morning. Should I phone you or nudge you?
7. Nice material. Wanna?
6. Excuse me. I seem to have dropped my Congressional Medal of Honor. Do you see it anywhere around here?
5. Excuse me. You have lipstick on your teeth.
4. Say, is that your toothbrush I see in your purse?
3. I'm the best and the worst thing that's ever happened to you.
2. That's a lovely blouse. It would look better on my floor.
1. Your eyes are like two vapid pools.

Stage Direction: Poly the Polygrapher walks to center of stage, carrying briefcase. She is dressed in appropriately intimidating attire (Leather mini, thigh-high leather boots, riding crop). She begins to set up. She calls for the first victim, uh, interviewee for a job. She explains to the audience that this is a confidential comedy sketch.

Poly: Alright, it's time for us to clear up just a few more questions. I think that we'll be able to cover them in this nineteenth session. Now let's just hook you up. *(Wraps victim with a reel of wires. Finally caps him off with deelyboppers.)* There. Is that comfortable?

First Subject: Well, no. But I'm starting to enjoy it. What are you doing after this?

Poly: Stay to the subject at hand. Now, get comfortable. Remember, this won't hurt.

First Subject: Ouch. I thought you said it wouldn't hurt.

Poly: Well, it won't hurt *me*. Now breathe normally.

First Subject: Okay. *(Gasping and wheezing from the nervousness, the wires, and her outfit)*

Poly: You're not *breathing normally!*

First Subject: Sorry.

Poly: Don't think about it, just do it! Now concentrate. Don't think about your breathing!

Alright, now let's go over these questions. You have the list right here. We've designed the instrument so that if you're not telling the truth, this buzzer will go off. *(buzz)* See?

Now, the first question. Have you used drugs recently?

First Subject: No. *(buzz)* Once, at a party. *(buzz)* Alright, what time is it now? *(no sound)*

Poly: What have you tried?

First Subject: Nothing. *(buzz)* Prescription medicine. *(buzz)* What have you got? *(buzz)* Alright, I'm addicted to Red Mercury. (*no sound*)

Poly: Now to the question of your judgment. Have you ever done anything that indicated that you have poor judgment?

First Subject: I joined the Directorate of Operations to get fast promotions. *(buzz)* I offered to testify against DCI Gates *after* he was confirmed. *(buzz)* I agreed to do this sketch. (no sound)

Poly: Have you ever mishandled classified information?

First Subject: Well, once I didn't give my correct badge number at the burn chute.

Poly: Do you have any financial difficulties?

First Subject: No. *(buzz)* Well, I lost big at the combination Coke dispenser/slot machine on the fourth floor. *(buzz)* Alright, I have a Congressional checking account.

Poly: Have you ever discussed classified material on the secure line?

First Subject: Huh?

Poly: Alright, I'll repeat it. Have you ever discussed unclassified material over an open line?

First Subject: Well, yes.

Poly: With whom?

First Subject: Well, I'm not sure. A lot of people.

Poly: Alright, we'll need their names. You'll have to come back later. *(First Subject exits.)*

Poly: Send in the next interviewee.

Alright, what's your name?

Second Subject: Bond, James Bond. (*To audience:* I've always wanted to say that!)

Poly: Who are you talking to?

Second Subject: Just the people out there.

Poly: I don't see any people out there. How long have you had these hallucinations?

Second Subject: Don't you see them?

Poly: Trying to deceive the polygrapher. This doesn't look good on your permanent record.

Let's move on to the next set of questions. Have you been unfaithful?

Second Subject: Why do you ask?

Poly: That's what I get paid for.

Second Subject: By the hour or the pound?

Poly: I don't get paid for *that*.

Second Subject: So much the better!

Poly: Hey, I'll do the punch lines around here! Back to the question. Are you faithful?

Second Subject: Yes.

Poly: Shucks.

Have you ever stolen anything?

Second Subject: Just the heart of every woman I've met.

Poly: I can see we're not getting anywhere. Let's discuss this afterwards.

(Second Subject exits.)

Poly: Please send in the next interviewee.

Alright, Mr. Perfect. It says here that you've had a perfectly boring life. In fact, you have no life. You don't drink, smoke, wench, and will only be doing unclassified work in the library. Now, let's get to the bottom of this flimsy sham. Have you ever stolen anything?

Perfect: Well, I think I left a pencil in my coat pocket once.

Poly: I see. And what number was it?

Pefect: I think it was a three. No, it must have been a two. Because I was taking one of your psych tests about whether I wanted to take a shower or eat pickled beets.

Poly: And what was your answer?

Perfect: I can't remember.

Poly: Why not? What are you trying to hide?

Perfect: Well, I guess I said the beets.

Poly: So you don't shower? What are you covering up? Time to come clean. We want all the dirt on you. And it looks like there's a lot of it.

Next set of questions. Have you had any foreign contacts?

Perfect: Well, my son's Boy Scout leader once talked to an Iranian. We've seen the Boy Scout leader once.

Poly: We want dates, times, places, and names. Come on. You'll have to do better than this.

Alright, next question. Have you ever disclosed classified material to anyone?

Perfect: Well, I once told my wife I liked my job.

Poly: And just how well do you know this wife of yours, if that is her real position?

Perfect: I'm sorry?

Poly: Sorry won't cut it here. Now, have you ever engaged in any subversive activities?

Perfect: I called G. Gordon Liddy's radio phone-in show.

Poly: I'm sorry, you won't cut it. Goodbye.

(He exits.)

Poly: Next. Now, your name is Patrick O'Lawlor?

Patrick: That's right.

Poly: What were you doing on St. Patrick's Day?

Patrick: I was wearing a green tie.

Poly: Does that mean you have ties to another power?

Patrick: No.

Poly: Do you then admit that you are working for the Irish Republican Army?

Patrick: No.

Poly: Then why the secret symbols? All this wearin' of the green? Do you admit that you once were seen drinking a beer at a pub?

Patrick: Why, yes.

Poly: And there were other people who liked Notre Dame's football team there?

Patrick: Well, I guess so.

Poly: Then you admit that you were meeting with Irish sympathizers. We can't have this. Goodbye.

(He exits.)

Poly: Next. Now, let's try just a few questions. Be as truthful as you can. Have you tried drugs?

Candidate: Yes, once. One of the Ochoa brothers asked me to fly a few loads into the Miami area.

Poly: Have you ever been in contact with a foreign intelligence service?

Candidate: Why, yes. I worked for the Soviets for several years.

Poly: Well, no deception indicated here. Welcome aboard.

Total Quality Management was the Next Big Thing among Agency managers for awhile, particularly in the Office of Leadership Analysis (LDA), where this skit was held during their Christmas party. The lead character was based upon the receptionist on Moonlighting, *in which she chirpily answered the phone with some cheery catch phrase.*
(Ring)

Terry? Hi. Glad I caught you. Sorry you're on vacation and couldn't make the holiday party. I thought I'd catch you up on what it's like being the stand-in LDA gatekeeper. You've missed all sorts of office developments. Wait a minute. Lemme just open this new Lotus Notes folder on it . . . Oh, excuse me a minute, the other line's ringing.
(Ring)

LDA—We empower analysis. You're a member of the Clinton transition team? Your previous experience was as Little Rock Drain Commissioner, so this stuff is pretty new to you? Well, you'll feel right at home here. What do we do? I'm sure you read our study of the candidates for the succession struggle on Pitcairn Island. Hello?

Terry? VIP Medical is doing well with the transition team and is getting really high-level access to the Oval Office. They're now taking specimens from presidential pet Socks' litter box.
(Ring)

LDA—We actualize potential. You say you want a Middle East bio? You've heard about this power behind the throne who runs everything? Ali Garchy? Hello?

Terry? USSR Division was moved even further away from the front office. But it sounded nice. Somewhere near Bermuda. I think they said something about Bermuda Triangle.

(Ring)

LDA—Where TQM is not just an alternative lifestyle. You're head of the CIS cluster? Well, I have good news for you. After three years, the Office of Soviet Analysis finally coordinated on that bio of Gorbachev's butler. Hello? Operator?

Terry? Yeah, as I was saying. The renovation is going fine. Bonnie's managed to get the junior analyst's office turned into that new Diet Coke cellar she'd been wanting.

(Ring)

LDA—Operationalize your visualization. You say you're from the downsizing task force? Sorry. Wrong number. Try the DDO.

Terry? You know, Rodney Dangerfield was given a tour through here and said, "Boy, this downsizing stuff is really tough. I can't get no recruitments. No recruitments at all. But it's tougher overseas. I saw a KGB guy outside with a sign: Will Spy for Food."

(Ring)

LDA—Seize opportunities to do opportunity analysis. You're from IBM? Yes, we're a PC office. Oh, you mean personal computers. I thought you meant . . . Hello?

Terry? The new computer LAN is almost ready. They figured learning all the new versions of AIM and LOTUS wasn't enough of a professional challenge, so they're dropping LOTUS for ROSE: Really Obsolete System for E-Mail. Yes, it's two tin cans with terminals at either end.

(Ring)

LDA—Putting INR/B where it should be. Transition team? You like our baseball cards with bios on them and were wondering if you could get Saddam Hussein's rookie card?

Terry? Twentieth Century Fox asked if they could use the renovation space to film Home Alone 3: Lost in A (corridor).

(Ring)

LDA—The little engine of change that could. You want to know if we have Prince Albert in a can? Bart Simpson, get off the line! Oh, it's you, sir. I thought we'd discussed these calls before, Mr. Quayle.

Terry? I managed to sneak into one of the corporate board staff meetings. They were doing one of their trust-building exercises. Looked more like a fraternity hazing to me. They went to a ropes course at Reston Town Center. Then the shrinks asked them about their feelings about their mothers. It was too weird for me.

(Ring)

LDA—Don't be the caboose in bottom-up evaluation. Mr. Heifetz? Baby! Loved your fiddle playin' at the New York Symphony. Oh, you're the other one? You do *what* for a living? You're going to Heifetz-ize us? Sir, that's still illegal in fourteen states!

Terry? Oh, it was just some obscene phone call. Which reminds me, I have to go to my polygraph appointment now. See ya.

The Memo Writers Strike Back

If It's Printed, It Must Be Legitimate

One of the guys in our office had just broken up with his girlfriend and was feeling down on himself. To spice up his life, I sent him a Valentine from an unknown admirer, with suitable come-on comments and Hershey's kisses as exclamation points for the message. I then recruited several folks throughout the building to send him similar cards, using different writing, different post offices, and, eventually, different countries of origin (thanks to a group of TDYers we brought into the campaign). It drove him nuts, but it seemed to restore his spirits. I've sat on the provenance of this story for two decades. If he buys this book, he'll finally know the truth of this venerable practical joke.

One of our colleagues' wives loved writing lengthy letters each day about local doings, taking advantage of the APO mail system. We obtained some of the APO letterhead and wrote her an official-sounding missive indicating that she had gone over the annual weight limit and there would be an exorbitant charge for all future mail.

In August 1981, when John McMahon ran the Directorate of Intelligence (the renamed NFAC), unnamed writers widely disseminated five NFAC Notices signed by "Ed McMahon." These appear in their original text, misspellings and all.

91

NFAC Notice   NFAC N 20-175
No. 20-175   05 August 1981
Reference: NFAC N 20-172

NFAC Reorganization

1. My initial call for a reorganization of NFAC has produced a response the likes of which I have never seen in my years of engineering managerial shakeups. The voluminous rumors that now abound were to be expected and are actually quite amusing, once you figure out which Office initiated them.

2. I am, however, a little nonplussed at the outright power grabs that are currently underway, as various NFAC officials both secretly and openly attempt to recruit employees for their new, "embryonic" domains. It is only slightly in jest that I remind everyone that kidnapping is a Federal offense, even on Agency grounds (DDO policy notwithstanding).

3. In light of the current activity, I have concluded that the reorganization cannot work as originally planned and I am proposing the following regroupment of NFAC into five regional Offices:

Office #1: Mountain Regions
Office #2: Plains Regions
Office #3: Coastal Regions (includes alluvial fans)
Office #4: Islands (smaller than Australia)
Office #5: Polar Regions (except Greenland)

4. We are currently writing up organizational descriptions for these areas. The number of slots in each Office has not been determined but I expect most OPA personnel will be assigned to Office #5. Most of their work tends to be highly polarized anyway, and, in fact, several OPA analysts have expressed to me personally their desire to do more research on the Poles.

—Ed McMahon

Infernal Use Only

NFAC Notice
This Notice Rescinds NFAC Notice 20-175

NFAC NOTICE   NFAC N 20-176
No. 20-176   6 August 1981

NFAC re-organization

1. Less than 24 hours after the announcement of the new NFAC plumbing chart, I am faced with the necessity of restructuring NFAC yet again. Over 90 percent of the NFAC analysts and supervisors immediately applied for jobs in Office #4: Islands—undoubtedly with the hopes of orientation trips to Tahiti, Fiji or Jamaica. Fat chance! I am not about to kill myself trying to wring more money out of Congress for foreign travel just so you turkeys can work on your suntans!

2. In have concluded, therefore, that the only fair and equitable organization of NFAC's offices is one based on the alphabet. Hence forward, all countries will be assigned to an office according to the first letter of the name, as follows:

Office #1: A through E (Afghanistan, Albania, Algeria, Angola, Antigua, etc.)
Office #2: F through J
Office #3: K through O
Office #4: P through T
Office #5: U through Z

3. Furthermore, in order to put an end to this insane raiding of the best analysts, all analysts and supervisors will be assigned to these offices according to the first initial of their last name. For example, Helene Boatman will have a choice of Bahrain, Bangladesh, Benin, Bolivia, or Burundi. Al Sapo-Box can choose between Office #1 and Office #4.

4. It strikes me that this organization solves another common complaint—that too many of our human resources are devoted to analysis of the USSR. Since few NFAC analysts have names beginning with the letter "U", we automatically solve the resource problem as well. Any analyst or supervisor whose last name begins with a letter for which there is no country has one week to legally change his or her name, after which pink slips will be tendered.

—Ed McMahon

NFAC notice   NFAC N 45-199
No. 45-199   6 August 1981

NFAC Reorganization—Logistics

1. As we proceed with plans for implementing the latest design for the reorganized NFAC, a few logistical problems have come to light. Desks, telephones, typewriters, and places to put them are admittedly petty concerns, but they are distracting analysts from the main business at hand—to get out the product.

2. Accordingly, I have proposed the following steps so that these difficulties can be overcome quickly:

(a) At 0900 on 1 September, all NFAC Personnel will report to the parking area in front of the Headquarters building. They will form up by country teams—Bolivia, Thailand, Libya, etc.

(b) At 0930 the fire alarm bell will sound. The various teams will then proceed to offices in the building they wish to have, establish defensive perimeters, and hold their territory. At COB, Front Office Personnel will come around and note room numbers. Our medical staff will carry away the wounded or critically disappointed.

3. Since certain teams—USSR, e.g.—will have numerical advantages, we will issue handicapping procedures prior to 1

September. The proposal to give USSR analysts the entire seventh floor has been rejected. On the other hand, if a seventh floor address is that important, I will change the signs so that all floors read "Seventh Floor".

4. In the past reorganization efforts have involved a certain amount of tinkering with walls, electrical outlets, and the like. To meet this problem I have ordered all interior walls in Headquarters Building removed. New telephones will be installed with extra-long cords. Desks will be mounted on wheels. All of this should contribute to greater inter-office communication and ease the process of implementing our next reorganization, planned for Summer 1983.

—Ed McMahon

Infernal Use Only

NFAC Addendum
NFAC Notice No. 20-176

NFAC Addendum   6 August 1981
No. 20-176 A

This addendum is for use with NFAC Notice No. 20-176. Paragraph No. 5 was inadvertently left off. Please be advised that paragraph 5 is noted below:

1. In keeping with our new alphabetical reorganization, I have decided to rename the National Foreign Assessment Center (NFAC). Beginning with this notice we will be called the Mixed Alphabet Analytic Center, or, "The Big MAAC." Thus, I will not have to change my name in order to remain Director.

Please note and make proper changes.

—Ed McMahon

NFAC Notice   NFAC N 45-200
No. 45-200   19 August 1981

NFAC Reorganization—Logistics

1. As we proceed with implementing the reorganization of NFAC, I wish officially to compliment those Offices that are entering on this venture with such unparalleled enthusiasm. I wish to single out the Office of Political Analysis for its especially praiseworthy attitude. In an earlier announcement I pointed out that OPA had spent only 10% of what it should have on outside contracts.

2. It gives me great pleasure to announce that within the last two days, the Office of Political Analysis has exceeded its budget for outside contracts. Most of these contracts are associated with the recently announced move of the Offices of Near East South Asia and Africa-Latin America to another building. The highlights of these contracts follow:

   —500 10-speed bicycles from Sears-Roebuck

   —6000 yards No. 3 twine, plus 150 No. 10 coffee cans for affixing at end of string to augment the existing communications system between the Operations Center and another building

   —Catered lunches by Macke & Sons vending corporation with a choice guaranteed of white bread or rye for all sandwiches (hold the mayo)

   —Feasibility study to install a "J.C. Penney-like" pneumatic tube system between Headquarters and another building

3. I realize that the move may have a short-term negative impact on our current intelligence responsibilities. I can assure you that we have anticipated this and are studying the latest high-technology means for assisting us in meeting our responsibilities. My interim plan is to contract with WTOP radio to broadcast 24-hour news to all our national security consumers. This "newzak" will be interrupted only periodically for the playing of another building's theme song "On the Road Again" by Willie Nelson.

—Ed McMahon

NFAC is not alone in the creation of counterfeit employee notices. The following three bulletins famously circulated surreptitiously in the Agency hallways, with the last one invoking the memory of Jonathan Swift's "A Modest Proposal":

Relocation Bulletin 19
1 September 1961

Toilet Facilities

1. During the early stages of the move to the new building, toilet facilities will not be available at the new site. However, all toilet facilities in the downtown area will remain in operation until the move is completed, at which time it is anticipated that all the toilet facilities in the new building will be activated. Upon activation of the facilities in the new building, the downtown toilet facilities will be rescheduled to provide for operation on Tuesdays and Thursdays, except national holidays.

2. Personnel assigned to the new building prior to the activation of all toilet facilities in the building will be expected to make personal provisions consistent with personal comfort. It is anticipated that prior to Christmas 1961 at least two temporary toilet facilities will be made available in the new building if funds permit. If and when installed, these temporary (for no longer than ten years) units will be located on the seventh floor adjacent to the public telephones and in the second sub-basement adjacent to the boiler room.

3. For security reasons personnel will not frequent gasoline stations, restaurants, and other public facilities in the vicinity of the new building with the intent of utilizing such toilet facilities, inasmuch as this will attract undue attention to Agency personnel.

4. Personnel are reminded that vegetation at the new building is U.S. Government property. Damage to or destruction of U.S. Government property is a Federal offense. Personnel are also reminded that some leaves of plants in adjacent wooded areas are harmful, such as poison ivy (3 leaves), poison oak, and poison

sumac. Photographs of these plants will be posted at the main entrance to the new building at an early date.

Distribution: All employees

Employee Bulletin

EB No. 11821   20 December 1984

Physical Security In The New Headquarters Building
    Several new procedures will be implemented by the Office of Security presently, which will enhance the physical security afforded to both the new and present Headquarters buildings. Several procedures to be instituted represent a radical departure from present security practices and all employees are encouraged to become familiar with them prior to implementation.

Description/Procedures
    a. On or about 24 January 1985, the construction crews will have completed the moat which surrounds both the construction site and the present Headquarters building. Designed to encompass the entire Headquarters compound at completion, the moat will serve as access control and enhance physical security present on completion of construction in 1987. Through an agreement with the National Zoo, approximately fifteen (15) live crocodiles will be installed in the moat, which has been constructed to accommodate heated water to support the crocodiles. Employees are cautioned not to venture closer to the moat than the warning signs indicate. The moat and its attendant features are to be serviced only by DA/PSB/MB (Moat Branch), a newly created office within the Directorate of Administration.
    b. On completion of the new Headquarters building, the Office

of Logistics will install land mines in all non-paved areas. This feature is expected to increase security in all outlying areas near and within the compound by reducing substantially the amount of traffic through non-paved areas. In addition, Logistics envisions the periodic creation of preformed planters in these areas to simplify planting of trees and new ground cover. Employees, especially joggers, are cautioned to obey the posted signs during the installation phase as the mines were procured from the Department of Defense as war surplus and occasionally are unstable. Applications for the installing crew may be obtained from OL, following execution of a waiver of coverage with Insurance Branch.

c. Plans to afford continuous helicopter patrols over the Headquarters compound have been cancelled. It was found that the maximum FAA-allowable flight ceiling (150 feet) would permit the helicopter patrols to become frequently entangled in the electrical wiring that surrounds the compound, negating their effectiveness. Alternative patrol plans are being investigated.

As further developments become available, periodic bulletins in this series will be distributed.

Distribution: all employees

Employee Bulletin

Personnel   99-86Q
                                                            13 June 1995

Agency Downsizing Incentive

As you are all aware, CIA has had to make dramatic cuts in spending to meet budget targets. To help up meet these targets, we are now looking for volunteers to commit suicide—this we believe will substantially reduce our salary bill.

Employees wishing to take part in this scheme are asked to

assemble on the roof of the South Tower NHB on alternate days from 1 October onwards. Participants will be given marks on the difficulty of their dives/jumps and the person with the highest score will receive enhanced death-in-service benefits. This action, in view of its voluntary nature, will not affect your pension rights.

Participants are asked to avoid landing on other employees or landscaping trees or shrubs, as this will cost more money than will be saved. Non-participants are asked to take extreme care on days when people will be jumping. Most people will be jumping from the South Tower, but other designated jumping spots will be Northwest Entrance OHB and the power plant roof.

All participants will be given the opportunity to change his/ her mind until they reach the jumping spots, after which it will be impossible for the attending officials to get into a catching position. Participants should also bring a large plastic bag into which your various bits will be placed after they have been picked up off the sidewalks. Anyone wishing to jump whilst inside the bag (to avoid unnecessary mess on the ground) will be given a bonus of Comp. Time.

You will be paid at your usual hourly rate while in the action of jumping, but all time cards must be signed off by your supervisor. Unfortunately, we cannot pay you for any practice jumps which you may undertake or any jumps undertaken outside of normal working hours. We are hoping to make a 45% cut in our salary budget through this scheme, but should it be undersubscribed, some mandatory jumpings cannot be ruled out.

Thank you for your cooperation.

The farewell book for DCI Robert Gates, *Bob Gates' Big Book of Humor,* featuring a DCI with a Snidely Whiplash mustache, consisted of blank pages.

When I was the head of an overseas facility, the U.S. Government had announced that henceforth smoking was banned from any and all U.S. Government installations. It was my responsibility to break the news to a very miffed cadre of smokers. After I sent out the requisite official USG memo, I sent out a second one, changing the word "smoke" to "fart." It was hilarious, broke the tension, and unruffled a lot of feathers.

In 2008, graphic designers created *Terrorist Illustrated: the Magazine Devoted to Promoting Fashionable Terrorism,* featuring bin Laden in a ball gown. Articles included:
—Exclusive: Usama Paints the Town-Save the Last Dance for Me
—50 Ways to Love Your 50 Wives
—The Doctor: Why You Should Always Stretch Before a Jihad
—How to Conceal Your Gun Under Your Gown
—Bonus Section: Exclusive Caves . . . Get Yours Before They're
   Gone

One of the most entertaining bio sheets was written by Leo Hazlewood, a senior Intelligence Community executive who served as the CIA's Executive Director and Deputy Director for Administration, and as the inaugural Deputy Director of the National Imagery and Mapping Agency, among other senior positions. Earlier, he would give audiences the following:

Mr. Hazlewood serves as Deputy Comptroller, a position he assumed on 1 July 1985. Since that time, numerous sources have reported seeing him wandering the halls wearing a green eye shade and carrying a hand calculator. Agency lore includes stories from program managers who were summoned to Mr. Hazlewood's cavernous office, which is illuminated only by the screen of a computer terminal, for close questioning about resource requirements.

Little is known about Mr. Hazlewood's background. An untested source reported that, when students in an Agency course asked about his experiences, Mr. Hazlewood commented "I was born; I entered on duty; and then I showed up for this course." Efforts to verify this report, or to obtain additional details about Mr. Hazlewood, have proved unsuccessful.

One of our summer hires was an accomplished restaurant reviewer. When he discovered a new hot dog machine in the basement of the Original Headquarters Building, he adapted his review to the Agency's style of memo writing and produced this gem:

Observations of OHB Hot Dog Machine

1. Location:
   - OHB Approximately GF45 near the elevators and green jacket hive (*Editor's note: the front office of the escorts for non-cleared personnel; all escorts wear their company's green jacket*)

2. Appearance:
   - Standard vending machine appearance with the words Oscar Mayer and a large wiener featured on front. Also includes observation window.

3. Features:
   Choice of 3 wieners, standard bun
   - Oscar Mayer wiener
   - Some German thing
   - Premium wiener with cheese core

4. Cost:
   - Oscar Mayer $2.00
   - The German $2.50
   - Premium cheese core $3.00

5. Extras—Requires manual assembly:
   - Ketchup

- Mustard
- No relish

6. Operation:
   - The hot dog vending machine appeared to operate correctly, serving a warm wiener assembled with a moist, slightly heated bun.
   - Multiple robotic mechanisms were observed through the observation window.
   - Robot 1 captured selected wiener (Oscar Mayer) from the wiener bay and positioned wiener in front of Robot 2.
   - Robot 2 was labeled with many hazard indicators suggesting it to have a heating function (*Field comment: heating could be powered by lasers*).
   - Robot 2 then opened its port to receive the wiener.
   - Robot 1 then inserted the wiener into Robot 2 for heating.
   - Robot 1 then proceeded to agitate the wiener in and out of Robot 2 until done—presumably when wiener had plumped.
   - Robot 1 then assembled wiener with a warm bun (nfi) appearing to rest in a Robot 3.
   - Robot 3 then delivered assembled hot dog through the serving port.

7. Taste:
   - Wiener had indeed plumped—characteristic splitting of wiener was observed. Wiener was thoroughly cooked and warm to the center.
   - Bun remained cooler and had not become soggy.
   - Quality equaled that of average Ball Park.

On December 23, 2003, the *Washington Times* reported that a December 17, 1974 White House Weekly Situation Report on

International Terrorism had been declassified. Buried in the true threat reporting was the following: "A new organization of uncertain makeup, using the name 'Group of the Martyr Ebenezer Scrooge,' plans to sabotage the annual courier flight of the Government of the North Pole. Prime Minister and Chief Courier S. Claus has been notified and security precautions are being coordinated worldwide."

Sometimes the external bureaucracy can get in the way. In 2000, the Red Cross ended its bimonthly blood drive at CIA because the FDA demanded that donors provide true name and travel histories, prompting one frequent donor to remark "We're ready to bleed for our country, but the bureaucrats won't let us."

Understanding DO and DI Writing

"The analysis came down firmly on both sides of the issue."
—Robert Gates, former DCI, describing a
1980 CIA assessment of Soviet intentions

"Electronic intercepts are great, but you don't know if you've got two idiots on the phone."
—Martin Peterson, former Executive Director

Sometimes the unsuspecting non-member of the Agency is able to learn enough of the acronyms to get by the first round of gatekeepers. But he or she is soon baffled by the jargon that Agency officers, in the trenches in the field and at Headquarters, use to obfuscate meaning and keep the riffraff out of the circle of knowledge. The following guides are often shared with rookie operations officers and analysts to help them in writing, respectively, cables and finished intelligence:

Guide to the New Reader of Headquarters and Field Cables

If the Cable Says	It Means
Headquarters encouraged by	You haven't done enough yet
Would appreciate	Do (want)
Request station	Do immediately
Please reply ref	Your next promotion is in jeopardy
As station is aware	Station doesn't know what follows

FYI Only	Don't tell your liaison drinking buddy
Alternate for F/1 is	If the dummy blows it the first time
Assume station has	We know you haven't yet
Please advise any Headquarters assistance necessary	Please do it yourself
Expert willing to TDY	1. Your own assessments stink; or 2. Expert wants a boondoggle
Request COS return for consultations	This is your last assignment; or You've done a good job
Will advise	Don't bug us; or Will not advise
Pugio in contact with	Pugio saw him at a cocktail party
Initial assessment favorable	He drinks
Wish recruit PRBLOOPER/ 1 as access agent to target	I need a recruitment before promotion time next month
Wish bring Headquarters up to date on	You missed the boat, dopes; or I've neglected reporting for six months
FNU Johnson	I was too drunk to get the name; or My pen went dry in the john
Request TDY assistance	Your project isn't important enough for one of our boys to do it
Concur ref plan	I don't understand what you're doing
Request bonus of $5,000	If we don't pay he'll quit; or If we don't pay he'll talk to the local service
Station unable to locate asset	Officer miscopied phone number
Suggest station consider	Ref plan is foul
High levels of the USG	The desk officer likes the cable
Highest levels of the USG	The branch chief likes the cable
Requires COS concurrence	It is impossible
Trace follows	The cable slipped through the crack
Results inconclusive	The guy's a fabricator, but he's the best we've got

Case officer unable	Case officer overslept
Proficient	Lousy
Adequate report	Three reports not disseminated; one report evaluated as satisfactory
Appreciate station efforts to date	You haven't done enough
Please relay	Originator of the cable was too stupid to send it himself
Liaison doesn't know of	Liaison is holding back information
Defer to Headquarters	We haven't a clue what to do now

Not to be outdone by their operational brethren, the analysts provided the following:

Guide to Reading DI Jargon in Intelligence Assessments

If the paper says	**It means**
It has long been known	I didn't look up the original cable
A definite trend is evident	These are practically meaningless
Of great theoretical and practical importance	Interesting to me
While it has not been possible to provide definite conclusions to these policymaker's questions	An unsuccessful analysis, but I still need to get it published
Three of the samples were chosen for detailed investigation through sensitive reporting	The results of the others didn't make any sense
Typical public opinion analyses show	The best results show
These results will be shown in a subsequent *PDB*	I might get around to this sometime if I'm pushed
The most reliable results are those obtained by Jones	He was my summer intern

It is believed that	I think
It is generally believed that	A couple of other guys think so, too
It is clear that much additional collection work will be required before a complete understanding occurs	I don't understand it
Correct within an order of magnitude	Wrong
Thanks are due to Joe for assistance with the methodologies and to George for valuable assistance	Joe did the work and George explained to me what it meant
A careful analysis of obtainable special intelligence	Three pages of notes were obliterated when I knocked over a glass of beer

In conclusion, it is clear that much additional collection work will be required before a complete understanding occurs. In this point of the analysis, these results are not statistically significant to generalize for the DI. However, the results are correct within an order of magnitude!

Most intelligence—raw, finished, or somewhere in between—has a dizzying set of classification barnacles attached to it. Among the most famous are Eyes Only. One variation was created for a briefing on Moshe Dayan, who had lost an eye in battle: Eye Only. Of course, this gem was also stamped Burn Before Reading, so that it did not fall into the wrong hands.

The sixteen members of the Intelligence Community have very distinctive cultures, as do the components within these agencies. Various DCIs, as part of their portfolio to ensure that the Community and the Directorates got along, stressed the values of "collaboration." DCI John Deutch referred to the Community as operating like a symphony, a metaphor that soon died when the appropriate sheet music could not be found. Other wags looked up the word "collaboration" in the dictionary, only to be reminded that in WWII, our OSS founders considered a "collaborator" to be "one who cooperates with the enemy," which explains a lot . . .

The Army Security Agency was not without its own specialized language. Somehow the editors missed that its nomenclature for a Chinese weapons system was also a slang term for sex organs. The term became part of official publications and remains in common use.

A senior DI officer was asked to coordinate on a DS&T publication based upon liaison reporting of camel-mounted anti-tank missiles. Apparently even liaison services have a sense of humor.

DCI Walter Bedell Smith called current intelligence, "First impressions (subject to) later revision."

In 2000, CIA analysts counseled each other, "don't make the same mistake once."

A self-impressed senior Chief of Station decided to send along unsolicited advice to the Chief of Station of a neighboring country. He prattled on and on about what sites to use, how to conduct countersurveillance, etc., essentially telling his peer how to suck eggs, something which *just isn't done* in the Clandestine Service. The recipient of this missive sent back a one-sentence reply: "Ref Cable is a wonderment!"

A sign posted in CIA's Central American Task Force in 1982:
Six Phases of a US Government Sponsored Covert Action:
Enthusiasm
Disillusionment
Panic
Search for the Guilty
Punishment of the Innocent
Praise and Honor for the Nonparticipants

If the Directorate of Intelligence was composed of high school cliques:

Political Analysts	Popular rich kids
Military Analysts	Jocks
Economists	Math nerds
Leadership Analysts	Chess club
Science, Tech, and Weapons Analysts	Audio/Visual geeks
Collection Analysts	Drama club
Targeteers	Gamers
Methodologists	Library kids
Graphic Designers	Goths

Humor as Political Indicator

Quips by Jon Stewart, Stephen Colbert, and late night comics aren't the only harbingers of what the public is really thinking. During the Cold War, when the Soviet Union and its satellites were "hard targets" that did not permit easy access to what the man on the street was thinking, the subjects covered by political jokes were sometimes used as indicators of underlying public opinion. Here are a few examples from behind the Iron Curtain:

East Germany (whose citizens often attempted to escape to West Germany)

—Did you know they are going to establish a new holiday next year? It's called the Day Commemorating Those Who Stayed Here!

—What is the definition of socialist absent-mindedness? When someone in our country stands in front of a store with an empty shopping basket and wonders if he was already inside or not.

—The new greeting in the German Democratic Republic is no longer "hello," but rather "still here?"

—Do you know why we will not need identity cards by 1991? By then, there will be only six people left, and Erich Honecker *(East German leader)* will know all of them personally. (*This later mutated into:* In 1992, all personal identification cards will have to be turned in, because everyone will know each other by then.)

—Erich Honecker had all the flowers taken out of his office because they have to be watered (the German word *giessen* means "to water") and he can't stand the word "Giessen" (also the name of the West German city where numerous East German emigrants were processed).

—What do East Germans like to eat the most? In the morning, Hungarian Goulash, afternoons, Wiener Schnitzel, and at night Bavarian Sauerkraut (in West Germany).

—There is a new disease in the GDR. It's called the Buda-pest ("pest" means "plague" in German).

—The German abbreviation for East Germany is DDR (*Deutsche Demokratische Republik*). It now stands for *"Der Doofe Rest"* (The dumb leftovers).

—What is the difference between Spain and the GDR? In Spain, the sun smiles over the whole country, but the whole world laughs at the GDR.

—For every emigrant leaving East Germany, the country gets one VW. No, not a Volkswagen, but a Vietnamese worker.

—It has been scientifically proven that East Germans could not have evolved from monkeys. Can you show me a monkey who can go without a banana for forty years?

—From the classified ads in an East German newspaper: "Will exchange a luxury apartment in East Berlin for a hole in the Wall."

—Students in East Berlin were getting a geography lesson. The teacher pointed to the map, saying, "Here is the Soviet Union, our friends. And here is the imperialist USA. And here is Africa, where wild people live in huts and are killing each other!" A student asked, "Do the wild people have a Communist Party?" "No." "Do the wild people have a Communist Workers' Union?" "No." "Do the wild people have Communist at all?" "No, they don't have communism." "Then what the hell has made them that wild?"

—An East German is caught by border guards trying to scale the Berlin Wall. He is sent to an insane asylum. When a relative visits him, she asks, "Why were you sent to the insane asylum?" "Because I wanted to immigrate to the Soviet Union."

Hungary

Question: Do you know what prizes the communists are now offering for recruiting new party members?

Answer: If you get one new member, you do not have to pay dues. Two new members, and you can quit the party. With three new members, you receive a certificate saying you have never been a member.

Romania

—Secret agents from the US, USSR, and Romania are discussing how state secrets are protected in their countries. The CIA officer says "My wife and I work at the CIA, and she has no idea about what I do, and I have no idea about what she's working on. Secrets are well protected." The KGB officer says, "Same in our office. My wife and I don't know what the other is working on." The Romanian Securitate agent tops them, saying "I work alone in my office and I have no idea about what I should be doing!"

—A Romanian shopper walks out of a bare store with an empty bag and says, "Now I can't remember if I was going to the shop or coming from the shop."

—A foreign secret agent is sent to Romania to assassinate communist leader Nicolae Ceausescu. He goes to a public meeting, aims, but the agent cannot shoot him. He tries several times but cannot do it. He returns to his headquarters, where his boss asks what happens. He says, "Whenever I managed to get into a good shooting position and was aiming, the whole crowd started shouting, 'Shoot him! Shoot him!'"

—A Romanian immigrant returns to Romania to visit his family. He walks out of the airport and thinks, "So many years, and I cannot believe I am back in Romania." He puts his luggage down and looks around with awe, "So many years . . . I cannot believe I am back in Romania." As he looks down to take his bags, he finds they have been stolen. "*Now* I believe I'm back in Romania!"

North Korea

—A North Korean citizen is walking down the street, loudly complaining about the poverty under Kim's regime, "We have no food. We have no warm water. We have nothing!" The police arrest him and drag him into the interrogation room. He is beaten up, and then they fire fake bullets at him to scare him with the noise. After he's terrified, the cops figure he'll be too scared to do anything again and let him go. He walks down the street, shouting, "We have no bullets. We have nothing!"

—Two North Koreans were wondering whether to defect to the United States. One warns, "I heard that in the US, two street dogs had eaten a guy!" His friend says, "Let's go, then. Yesterday in Pyong'yang I saw two guys sharing only one dog!"

USSR

—An actual news story from the *New York Times:* An officially designated Hero of the Soviet Union used his privileged status to order a large quantity of furniture on a preferential basis from the Red October Furniture Factory in Yaroslavl. The Factory told him he would have to wait only seven years for delivery. The man was eighty-five years old. *Sic transit imperium.*

—Brezhnev was proud of a new postage stamp with his picture on it. But after a few months, the KGB noticed that the stamps were not showing up on the mail that they were opening. So they conducted a survey. Fifty percent of the stamps were losing their glue because the users were licking its backside too enthusiastically. The other 50 percent of the people were spitting on the wrong side of the stamp.

—A Russian citizen was throwing anti-communist leaflets on the Red Square in Moscow. He was arrested by the KGB and questioned as to why the papers were all blank. He said "It's obvious, anyway. Why should I write it down?"

—What is three hundred meters long, ten meters wide, and eats vegetables? The salami queue in front of the Moscow supermarket.

—What is a Soviet trio? A quartet returning from an overseas tour.

—Cosmonaut Yuri Gargarin leaves a note for his wife. "Dear Natasha. I'm going to outer space. I'll be up in the sky. Will be back on Monday." After landing, he returns to his home to find a note from his wife, "Dear Yuri. I'm waiting in the bread line. I have no idea when I will be home."

—In a Soviet school, the teacher was going on about the importance of work and asked young Yevgeny where his dad worked.

"He is a doctor"

"Yevgeny, please come sit in the front row. And Vladimir, where does your father work?"

"He is a university professor."

"Oh, that is very good as well. Please take a seat in the front row, too. And Boris, what of your father?"

"He works in the KGB's interrogation section."

"Um, er, yes. Yevgeny, Vladimir, back row, now! Boris, please sit in my chair!"

—Archaeologists at a major dig found a mummy in Egypt. Scientists the world over questioned how old it could be. After examination in the US, American scientists estimated it was 3,000 years old. It was then sent to Tokyo. After Japanese scientists looked at it with their more precise methods, they said it was 2,953 years old. It then was sent to Russia for examination. The Soviets announced, "The mummy is 2,953 years, five months, two weeks, and four days old." Journalists asked how they determined this. The Soviets replied, "It confessed under KGB interrogation."

—In the Moscow subway, someone asks, "Excuse me, comrade, do you work for the police?" "No." "Are you a member of the Communist Party of the Soviet Union?" "No." "Do you work for the KGB?" "No." "Is anyone in your family affiliated with the Soviet government?" "No, I am just a simple citizen." "Then get the hell off my foot!"

—At morning muster, KGB Moscow agents were told "Please do not let anyone pee in the park. Our microphones are getting rusty."

—A Russian visits the Lenin mausoleum in the Kremlin. He says to the guard, "I want to talk to Lenin." The guard says, "He's dead. He's lying in his coffin in the mausoleum." The Russian returns the next day, with the same request. The guard shouts "Lenin is dead! He can't hear you nor talk to you, so go home, comrade!" The Russian comes back the third day, with the same request. The guard yells, "Pay attention! Lenin is dead! Why do you keep repeating this question?" The Russian says, "Because it's so good to hear that he's finally dead!"

The Jews in USSR were subjected to particularly brutal harassment by the KGB and other representatives of Soviet authority, but their humor shone through.

—Someone knocked on Shapiro's door at 3 am. He tried to ignore it, but the knocker wouldn't go away. He answered the front door by asking, "Who is it?"

"The postman."

Shapiro opened the door, finding five KGB agents awaiting him with the question, "Tell us, Shapiro, what is the greatest country in the world"

"Our homeland, of course."

"And what is the best political system yet invented?"

"Communism."

"And in what country do the workers enjoy real freedom?"

"The USSR."

"Then why, Shapiro, have you applied to emigrate to Israel?"

"Because at least there the postman doesn't wake you up at 3 am!"

—Shapiro applied to emigrate out of the Soviet Union. He was called to the local immigration office, OVIR, and told that his application had been turned down. "Why?" asked Shapiro.

"Because you know state secrets from your workplace," replied the OVIR functionary.

"State secrets? Hah! In my field, the US is at least twenty years ahead of us."

"Yes, Shapiro, but that *is* the secret!"

—Shapiro applied to emigrate to Israel and was called in to OVIR, whose representative asked, "Isn't everything good for you here? Don't you have all that you need?"

Shapiro answered, "I have two reasons to emigrate. First, my neighbor comes home drunk every night, cursing the Jews. He says that as soon as the Communists are overthrown, he and his Russian buddies will go out and hang all the Jews."

"But Shapiro, you know that the Communists will never be overthrown."

"Yes. That is my second reason!"

—Brezhnev and Kosygin were discussing the Jewish Question. "Kosygin, how many Jews are in the Soviet Union?"

"Maybe two and a half million."

"And if we opened the borders to let out the troublemakers among them, how many do you think would leave?"

"Tops, no less than five million."

—The pollsters were called in again to conduct an international comparative survey of an American, an Israeli, a Pole, and a Soviet. "Excuse me. We're conducting a poll on the shortage of meat in your country" the pollster said to each.

"What's a 'shortage'?" asked the American.

"What's 'excuse me'?" asked the Israeli.

"What's 'meat'?" asked the Pole.

"What's a 'poll'?" asked the Soviet.

—Marxist theory calls for many transitional stages in history. What is the necessary transitional stage between socialism and communism? Alcoholism.

—Name history's first Communists. Adam and Eve—they walked around naked, had one apple between them, and thought they lived in Paradise.

—What are the four things wrong with Soviet agriculture? Winter, spring, summer, autumn.

—What do the US and USSR have in common? The ruble is worthless in both countries.

—An American tourist walks into a Moscow butcher shop and says to the clerk, "I'm giving a party tonight for some friends. Please wrap up ten steaks."

"Delighted to. Give me the steaks."

—What is the ratio between a dollar, a pound, and a ruble? In Odessa, a pound of rubles is worth a dollar.

—Define a Soviet string quartet. A Soviet symphony orchestra that has returned from a tour of the West.

—What's the difference between a Soviet optimist and a Soviet pessimist? A Soviet optimist studies English. A Soviet pessimist studies Chinese.

—What is the difference between Catholicism and Gorbachev's communism? Catholicism has life after death. Gorby's communism has posthumous rehabilitation.

—What is an exchange of opinion in the CPSU (Communist Party of the Soviet Union)? It's when I come to a party meeting with my own opinion, and I leave with the party's.

—Brezhnev was vacationing at his Crimean dacha. He woke up, went to the balcony, and greeted the sun. "Good morning, beautiful sun! What a beautiful day it is going to be!"

The sun replied, "Good morning, revered First Secretary of our beloved Party!"

Around noon, he exited his office and went to his garden, looked up, and addressed the overhead sun. "Good afternoon, dear sun!"

"Good afternoon, courageous hero of the anti-fascist war and beloved first citizen of our glorious homeland," the sun replied.

Brezhnev finished his work for the day and went back to his balcony to greet the sunset. "Good evening, setting sun."

"Go to hell, dirt bag. I've made it to the West!"

—The KGB, the FBI, and the CIA are all trying to prove that they are the best at apprehending criminals. The President decides to give them a test. He releases a rabbit into a forest and each of them has to catch it.

The CIA goes in. They place animal informants throughout the forest. They question all plant and mineral witnesses. After three months of extensive investigations, they conclude that rabbits do not exist.

The FBI goes in. After two weeks with no leads they burn the forest, killing everything in it, including the rabbit, and they make no apologies. The rabbit had it coming.

The KGB goes in. They come out two hours later with a badly beaten bear. The bear is yelling: "Okay! Okay! I'm a rabbit! I'm a rabbit!"

Armed with this knowledge, various members of the Intelligence Community could come to different conclusions, phrased with their own unique language, when asked "Are the Russians coming?"

George Kennan thinks the Russians are coming and may be here tonight.

The Air Force believes the Russians have the capability to come and have preplanned missions to do so at any time.

The Defense Intelligence Agency thinks the Russians are coming but probably won't be here until sometime next week.

Army agrees with DIA.

CIA thinks the Russians would like to come here but has no

opinions as to when they might wish to arrive.

The State Department's Bureau of Intelligence and Research believes the Russians love us and have no wish to come here.

Marshall Shulman knows the Russians are coming and wants to head the welcoming committee.

The Arms Control and Disarmament Agency (ACDA) has identified the true enemy—us.

Admiral Stansfield Turner (Director of Intelligence at the time of this joke) thinks the Russians are coming but won't be able to verify it for another four years.

The National Security Agency will not believe the Russians are coming until they hear them.

The National Photographic Interpretation Center will not believe the Russians are coming until they see them.

NOSIC has the true story but won't tell because nobody's cleared.

The FBI has no opinion.

The US Secret Service believes the Russians are coming, but doesn't really care because they've never threatened the President.

The Navy doesn't know but disagrees with everybody.

The Marines believe the Russians are already here and are running the Pentagon.

The Office of Management and Budget believes the Russians are coming and will fund our response in next year's budget.

The National Security Council believes the Russians are coming and that it is time to beat the hell out of them.

A KGB officer brings pictures of an Arab diplomat in flagrante with a woman. The Chekist asks what the Arab proposes to do with the picture. He replies, "Can I have them in color as well as glossy black and white?"

Family Ties

My father was a senior Agency officer, and I followed in his footsteps from almost before I could walk. He had taken a lot of time when telling me that he was Agency, explaining that it was not like the movies. He said that all he did was meet people and write reports. I learned earlier than most Agency children what my dad really did. When a local war broke out, my mother was in another country with my sisters and was evacuated to a third country, leaving me alone in the war zone with my dad. He, of course, had to work 24/7 so he decided to bring me to the office to stay during the crisis. As we were leaving the house, he asked my help in taking some things from a locked section of the house to the car. Out came all kinds of spy equipment: disguise kits, water soluble paper, weapons, and gadgets I did not recognize. I was shocked, thrilled, amazed, and shouted to my father, "Dad, you lied to me. It really is like the movies!" To which my father responded, "Shut up and load the car, dammit!"

At Family Day at CIA Headquarters (an annual event in which we can bring in our family members to show them where Daddy/ Mommy works), an Agency officer brought in his twelve-year-old son and ten-year-old daughter. He was showing his children an unclassified exhibit in one of the hallways, which featured several technical gadgets from long-ago clandestine operations. He son asked, "Dad, were you ever involved in any of these Top Secret operations?" The father smiled and used the old line: "Aw, if I tell you that, I'll have to shoot you." The boy immediately pointed at his sister and said, "Tell her!"

A group of case officers had some TDY visitors from Headquarters. When one of the visitors heard a female case officer was working at the station, he burst out with "she gives the sex in the DO." One of the case officers standing there was her husband.

Security and Cover

A colleague who served with the Special Services Unit, the 1946 bridge between the World War II-era Office of Special Services and the 1947-and-beyond Central Intelligence Agency, offers his reminiscences of an ongoing problem for those trying to live their covers:

I was present at the creation: SSU in 1946, when as a first lieutenant I was adjutant in the War Department Detachment, the cover name for SSU Headquarters in Heidelberg. Munich is about 150 miles from Heidelberg, but in 1946 transportation by a weatherized Jeep took about four hours with bridges out on the Autobahn, fords across creeks, and other obstacles here and there. German civilian transport by regular-sized automobiles was meager to non-existent, propelled by a sort of apparatus, known as a gasogen, mounted on the rear bumper, which managed a destructive distillation of wood, using whatever it was that resulted to run the engine. Interesting.

My Jeep was better transport, but it took the usual time for me to make a courier run to Munich Base late one autumn afternoon. The clue to base location was that headquarters was in a large house in the English Garden, somewhere near the VD Hospital. I arrived after dark in a pouring rain, but managed to locate the English Garden, a huge downtown park. The streets were empty and dark—street lighting was practically non-existent—and the VD Hospital was not immediately obvious. As I drove slowly and aimlessly around in the rain, a young German crossing the street loomed in the headlights. He stopped and came over to the side of the Jeep as I blinked my lights and yelled. Meanwhile, not wanting, as an American, to ask a German where the VD Hospital was, I had a bright idea. After I greeted the man in my badly fractured German, he smiled, and said in English almost without accent, "It's all right. What can I do for you?" Much relieved, I executed the brilliant idea, and asked, "Do you know of any place nearby where there are a lot of automobiles parked?" Again he smiled, and replied, "Why, yes. You must mean the headquarters of the American Secret Service." Somewhat rattled at that, I gave him a weak, "Yes," and received accurate directions, with landmarks I could see in the rain. I never did see the VD Hospital.

A counterintelligence officer is someone who looks at himself in the mirror every morning and thinks, "I wonder who that man is working for."

Sen. Barry Goldwater, suggesting that Congress should not increase its oversight of the CIA, quipped, "There are more leaks here than in the men's room at Anheuser-Busch."

Congressional oversight can be dicey at times, when representatives not familiar with the arcanae of intelligence sometimes have difficulty following a briefing. John Maury, CIA legislative counsel in the 1970s, recalled that one member did not know the difference between Libya, Lebanon, and Liberia. Another, who was shown a chart of covert action initiatives, asked "What the hell are you doing in covert parliamentary operations?!" The chart said "paramilitary operations." Mollified, he said "The more of these, the better. Just don't go fooling around with parliamentary stuff. You don't know enough about it."

—Quoted by John Ranelagh, author, *The Agency*

Here's yet more guidance from our colleagues in the armed forces:

The Fifteen Commandments of Operational Security

I.   Thou shalt not park thy helicopter in the open, for it bringeth the rain of steel.

II.   Thou shalt not expose thy shiny mess gear, for it bringeth unwanted guests to chow.

III.   Thou shalt not wear white T-shirts, or thine enemies will dye them red.

IV.   Thou shalt provide overhead concealment, for thine enemies' eyes are upon thee.

V.   Thou shalt cover thy tall antenna, for fly swatters groweth not in yon wood.

VI.   Thou shalt use a red lens on thy flashlight, or it shall appear as a star in the East.

VII.   Thou shalt cover the glass on thy vehicle, for the glare telleth thine enemy thy location.

VIII.   Thou shalt blend with thy surroundings, for trees groweth not in yon desert.

IX.   Thou shalt cover the tracks of thy vehicle, for they draweth pretty pictures.

X.   Thou shalt cover thy face, hands, and helmet, for thine enemies maketh war not on bushes.

XI.   Thou shalt not drape thy net on thy tent, for it looketh like tent draped in net.

XII.   Thou shalt hide the wires of thy commo, for they pointeth to thee.

XIII.   Thou shalt practice the art of dispersion, or one round will finish you all.

XIV.   Thou shalt pick up thy trash and litter, for they exposeth thy presence.

XV.   Thou shalt conceal the noise of thy generator, for thine enemies are listening.

Editor's Note: commo is communications gear.

This story is courtesy of a former CIA Office of Security officer who served overseas:

In the mid 60s, I accepted an invitation to a party hosted by a senior State Department officer who was a friend of mine and with whom I had considerable interaction. He lived in a large home in the suburbs.

About an hour into the party, I needed to use the facilities. I headed for the front door, knowing that most large Thai homes had a small guest bathroom consisting of a toilet, sink, and mirror just off a hallway leading from the front door to the rest of the house. Spotting a door in the hallway that I suspected led to the guest bathroom, I tried the door handle. It was unlocked and I stepped inside. Much to my horror, directly in front of me was the host's wife, an attractive fortyish blond, whom I had never met before, sitting on the toilet, looking at me. She gasped, as did I. Thoroughly rattled, I reached down to pat her on the head, I suppose a sort of consoling measure (as in, "There there, I'm getting out of here and I have seen nothing other than the color of your drawers and I won't say anything to anybody." Clearly a lie now that I think about it). After a couple of head pats, I raised my hand and turned to leave. Unfortunately, I found that I had a large blond wig in my hand. Apparently, a hair clip had somehow got caught under my ring. Sitting there now with her wig gone, her normal hair all plastered down and tucked in what appeared to be a little skull cap, perhaps fashioned out of a piece of panty hose, she gasped again. I then proceeded, totally out of control, to plop the wig back on her head. Finding that it was on crooked, I made a futile attempt to straighten it, only to make it worse, before fleeing the scene. The really remarkable thing was that no words were spoken between us, just gasps and odd strangulating sounds emanating from deep in the throat.

I then debated whether to abort the party or see it through. The finger foods being particularly delicious, I elected to stay.

The hostess eventually emerged, looking very shaken, with eyes maniacally shifting back and forth throughout the guests. I saw when she spotted me, somehow managing to avoid actual eye contact. From that point on, wherever I was in the room, she would be in a position that represented the furthest she could possibly be from me.

I was in the country for another couple years and saw her at numerous social events, always as far away from me as possible, looking a little rattled, probably 'cause she had to pee and was afraid to go to the bathroom. I suspect she never told her husband, as he and I remained good friends and he showed no signs of discomfort. Besides the locking of doors, the apparent moral is not to wear rings at social events.

Security shows up in other rooms of the house:

The Director of the Office of Security was one of several senior officers who attended a DCI-hosted offsite. Some very senior officers had private rooms; the others had to double up with colleagues. The Director of Security was known to snore, loudly and heartily, and his roommate worried that he would not be able to sleep that night and would show up the next morning worse for wear and embarrass himself in front of the Director and the assembled worthies. To everyone's surprise, then, the roommate showed up to the first morning meeting well-rested, whereas the Director of Security looked bedraggled and bloodshot. At breakfast, when asked how this was possible, the roommate said, "It's simple. When I tucked him in, I kissed him goodnight. He stayed wide awake, on his side of the room, all night!"

Same room, new story:

DCI Dick Helms visited us on the way to his honeymoon in

Jamaica. Meetings with Case Officers and Staff were held locally. The Chief asked me to stay in the safe house (SH) with the Director and his new wife Cynthia overnight, in the event anything untoward happened. The SH was configured with three bedrooms; the master room had two single beds. The following morning, the Chief arrived early, we had breakfast with the Director and his bride, and then escorted them to the airport for his flight to Jamaica. Prior to leaving for the airport, I took the SH keeper aside and instructed her to only make-up one bed in the master bedroom, leave the other as is, then take the rest of the day off. As was predictable, the Chief wanted to return to the SH to do a walk thru to determine no personal or classified material was left behind. He noticed only one of the twin beds was used in the master bedroom and immediately assumed the Director and Cynthia used that small bed all night. At that point he called Headquarters to inform Senior Staff of the Director's activities.

The Office of Security in the 2000s issued electronic fobs that hung off one's badge lanyard. The fobs generated a random six-digit passcode that was to be used by the officer as an adjunct to one's personal password when logging in to the system. The fobs eventually disappeared, but not before staffers learned that they were excellent generators of poker hands.

The fobs also tended to scrape against one's badge photo. One senior officer proudly displayed the horns that the fob had worn into his headshot.

Security awareness can't start at too young an age. When my daughter was working for the Agency during a summer, she came home all excited. When we sat down to dinner, my wife asked, "So, how was your first day?"

"I'm sorry, but I can't talk about it. You're not cleared. But Dad, after dinner's over, we've got to talk. Wait'll you hear these stories!"

Two blonde spies on separate missions in Eastern Europe joined up to cross the Alps and escape to neutral Switzerland. They were beginning to feel safe finally and so one spy started to tell the other about the secret information he had discovered. The other spy, blonder than the first, said, "Shush!" and looked around worried. "What's wrong?" asked the first spy. "We're safe! There's no one around for miles!" The worried spy said, "I'm not talking until we get to our contact. Haven't you heard of *mountain-ears?*"

The Deputy Director for Intelligence was having dinner with several couples when the Director of Security asked him to drop everything and come in to Headquarters. He arrived to meet two FBI agents with photocopies of a map of China with air routes, a sheet with characteristics of a US bomber, and a Secretary of Defense letter to the DCI. All but one of the documents—a Jewish marriage license—suggested that there was a planned attack on a Chinese nuclear facility. The DDI noted that the letterhead and other aspects of the SecDef letter indicated that it was a forgery. The map was only a map. The characteristics of the bomber could easily be found in the latest edition of *Jane's*. Although the marriage license was authentic, the others were not. The relieved FBI agents went on their way, and the DDI returned to finish his dessert. Days later, it was discovered that it was part of a draft spy thriller. The documents were an annex that was to appear in a pocket of the book cover. The documents had been found in the trash can of a hotel in Asbury Park, New Jersey. There is no intelligence that the E Street Band was involved.

One of the Agency's older buildings had a controlled documents area. One had to go through turnstiles and present identification to an armed guard to get into the area. One night, I came to the very quiet building and found that the guard was asleep. I carefully lifted myself over the turnstile, crept past the guard, let myself into the area, did my research, wrote my finished intelligence piece, and reported the guard the next day. The result? Just before retirement, I was charged with a security violation for unauthorized entrance to the facility.

A Security officer was sent on a long TDY to Moscow. Upon arrival, he was told that he would be followed everywhere he went, as the Russians were more interested in "visitors" than the PCSrs. He liked to explore, so he spent a lot of time walking around, getting to know the city. One day he decided to explore Gorky Park, with two tails in tow. He ended up getting lost. After passing the same spot several times, he got fed up and walked back to the tails, acknowledged their presence, and asked them if they could direct him back to his hotel. They not only acknowledged him but walked him back to the hotel and tipped their hats as they left him there.

Essays and Poems

Some topics inspire us to wax lyrical, poetic, or just passionate with prose. Here are a few of the more popular efforts that circulated in the Headquarters hallways:

Burn Bags

Many different elements, from the small to the significant, contribute to the CIA's ability to function. These disparate ingredients include our Dinosaur Delta Datas and Wonderful Wangs word processors, our legions of PhDs, our well-stocked library, and our intensely loyal workforce. But there is one indispensible item that ties us together and keeps the Agency running—the burn bag.

Almost every experienced Agency employee can recall an amusing anecdote or an unfortunate episode relating to these containers for our classified trash and various forms of non-toxic (?) waste. For some, like myself, burn bags even provide a pleasant physical experience. I refer to the sensation produced by dropping a bag down a chute in the OHB. You are rewarded with a whoosh of air that blows your hair back, not unlike the feeling you get when you stick your head out the window of a car moving at about 25 miles per hour.

Ironically, the literature of burn bags is paper thin. My research in the Agency library has not turned up any articles, essays, odes, or even limericks written in celebration of this ever-present part of our professional lives. Consequently, I can only impart my personal reflections about the bag.

Burns bags, I believe, should be treated with care and respect. Thus, I am distressed by the way a lot of people staple their bags. I always fold the top over twice so that the bag looks nice and so that there is enough paper to give the staples something to bite on. I also like to make two neat rows of staples, one over the other, so that the bag will not pop open and reveal my waste to the world. Two rows of staples is actually a lot; I counted twenty-seven staples on my last full bag. That may seem excessive, but I do not recall anything about staple restrictions during my EOD security lecture.

I remember one poor soul who only used four staples. His bag did not even make it to the chute. It spilled all over his cart. For punishment, his Security Officer sentenced him to eat a "super dog" in the cafeteria every day for a month. He lasted sixteen days, and then he collapsed in the waiting room of the Office of Medical Services. Three days later, when his name was called and he did not answer, OMS launched a search and eventually found his body curled up next to a May 1972 *Reader's Digest*. His death was attributed to an acute ingestion of bone meal and plastic.

Trashmanship

Some people never go to the burn bag chute. But they never have a full burn bag in their workplace, either. They usually fit one of two profiles. The first has on-board radar. As soon as you get up to take your burn bag to the chute, s/he pipes up, "As long as you're going to the chute, could you take my bag, too?" It is difficult for most of us "can do" commandos to turn down such a request, especially if there *is* room on our cart.

The other type is much more insidious. This is the person who, when no one is looking, takes his/her burn bag and puts it out in the middle of the corridor or in someone else's cubicle. When you arrive at work one morning, you discover a trove of twenty-five burn bags in the place where you thought you had a popcorn popper. Fortunately, you can usually identify this culprit by making a careful analysis of his/her bag-stapling technique. Like fingerprints and snowflakes, no two staple jobs are alike.

It Wasn't Yves St. Laurent

I have always wondered who designed the burn bag with the red-stripe design on the side. I assume that the striped bag is supposed to prevent you from confusing it with your Safeway lunch bag, thereby ensuring that you do not cart home most of the shredded economic secrets of Bangladesh.

I fondly recall the time several years ago when the supply of pinstriped bags mysteriously ran out and—appropriately in many case—dog food and fertilizer bags were rushed into the breach. You could cram a lot more trash into them, but, if you filled them, Hulk Hogan could not lift them.

Read Before Burning

Those substitute bags raise an interesting point. Why couldn't the Agency sell advertising space on its regular burn bags? It could make some money, and it also could provide a valuable service for its employees. If the Office of General Counsel's legal eagles could not agree to selling outside advertising, however, the bags could be adorned with messages on current topics of interest to employees. For example, everyone would read an explanation about why anybody below SIS rank has to park in the West A Loudoun County lot and walk from there. Or why, in an edifice as imposing as the New Headquarters Building, there are only about two conference rooms, each as large as a small shoebox, while the lobby is large enough to relocate the threatened Brazilian rain forest.

More Burning Questions

It was never fully explained to me why ripping your classified trash in two constitutes proper disposal. Why not rip it in three? Why rip it at all? Someday, I would like to go down to the big room in the sub-sub-sub-basement and get a tour of the shredder. How does it work? Did I mess up the machine that time I put a banana peel in my burn bag? And what about the time I got mad at my boss and sent his Northern Virginia phone book down the chute?

Does our classified trash really end up as insulation? I think we could do better financially if we packed it up and sold it as Top Secret Tidbits. Our sales would help the local economy, because everybody knows that the only people who buy that kind of stuff have names like Duke and Twila and come from Council Bluffs, Iowa.

Why do we have to make a burn bag run to the basement of the New Headquarters Building when there is a burn bag chute right down the hall? According to one story, the contractors for the NHB thought that they were putting in laundry chutes—the Security people would not tell them what the chutes were for, because they did not have a "need to know"—so they did not make heavy-duty chutes. As a result, every time a burn bag takes the fatal plunge, it destroys the chute, causing it to be closed for a couple of months until repairs can be made. I would like to have *that* service contract.

Beaucoup Bags in the Bowels

The subterranean burn bag room, of course, is not identified as such. Once you stumble upon it, you feel a bit like Indiana Jones discovering the Temple of Trash. There are orange-ish sort of dumpsters lined up all the way down that room, and each is overflowing with burn bags. And then the Keeper informs you that you are viewing a one-day accumulation. This sight can produce intense feelings of guilt. If you are only filling one measly bag a week you must not be pulling your share of the weight.

In my case, however, guilt quickly gave way to greed. I calculated the value of the contract to supply all of those bags. Administrations come and go, but the bags will just keep piling up and up until paper is eliminated. That may happen eventually, but for now I am going to hang on to my Conserva-files. Meanwhile, I may transfer to the DA's Burn Bag Division to get closer to the action. And when I retire, I do not want a medal. I only want one thing—the burn bag contract.

Ode to a DI Editor

Although the Agency hires brilliant people, their products are not individual products, signed by them, but rather a corporate guesstimate of what's going on in the world. As such, nothing gets the Agency's imprimatur without being handled by several levels of editorial review. Many DI analysts believe that the trick to success is getting into a level of the Agency that puts you in the hands of an even number of editors. The first editor changes your piece 180 degrees from what it was. The second editor changes it 180 degrees from that, or word-for-word precisely back to the piece you originally wrote!

This time-honored tension between editor and analyst led one of the analysts to pen this Seuss-style classic:

Every analyst at Langley liked writing a lot,
But the *SEIB* editor, who worked deep inside Langley, did
    not.
He hated writing—the whole writing process.
Now please don't ask why, no one quite knows in his office.
It could be frustration at endless rough drafts.
It could be, perhaps, the numerous gaffes.

But, I think that the most likely reason of all
May have been that his patience was two sizes too small.

But whatever the reasons,
The drafts or the gaffes,
He sat at his desk hating his staff.
Storming out from his desk, like a crook on a caper

At the analysts working away on their papers.

For he knew every analyst at Langley, you see,
Was busy checking their draft for submittal by three.
"They're not using their spell checks," he snorted with a sneer.
"The deadline's approaching. It's practically here."

Then he growled, his frustration growing and stirring,
"I must find some way to stop mistakes from occurring."

For soon, he knew, his analytical staff
Would hit the SAVE key and forward their drafts.
And then, oh, the mistakes, the mistakes, the mistakes.
If there's one thing he hated, it was the mistakes.

They'll hyphenate leftwing, lameduck, and gunman.
They'll write out all numbers from one million to ten.
They'll capitalize Wars when none were declared,
Or the word Party when the full name is not there.

Government, too, will get a big "G",
Even if not combined with Laos or Fiji.

They'll use graphics when a simple bullet would do.
They'll fill up a page with no white space in view.
They'll use acronyms without spelling them out.
So many mistakes I just want to shout.

Then the analysts, young and old, would sit down at their
  desks
And they would moan about the feedback they'd get.

And they'd moan, moan, moan, moan.

They would moan that their style was learned way back in
    school
Which was something that he couldn't stand from these
    fools.
And the more he thought about this writing routine
The more he thought, "I must stop this whole thing."
"For thirty-three years I've put up with it now.
I must stop mistakes from occurring, but how?"

Then he got an idea.
A brilliant idea.
He got a wonderfully brilliant idea.

"I know just what to do," he laughed to himself
And took some *Style Guides* from off of the shelf.
"What a brilliant idea," he heard himself say.
"I'm now certain to get a nice EPA."

Then he ran out into the main office space,
Where the editor sat, a smile on his face.

The desks were all empty, the analysts not seen
Having all stepped away to vending machines.
When he came to the first desk by the Xerox machine,
"This is stop number one," he said to thin air,
And threw the *Style Guide* on the analyst's chair.
Then he left a *Style Guide* with each of his staff.

And raced back to his office to chuckle and laugh.
"Pooh Pooh, to the analysts," he sang like a song.
"They'll find out about now that their style is all wrong.
They're just getting back! I know what they'll do.
Their mouths will hang open a minute or two.

Then the analysts at Langley will all cry 'Boo Hoo.'"
"That's a noise," grinned the editor,
"That I simply must hear."

So he paused and put his hand to his ear
And heard a sound rising from the main space.
It started out low, but soon grew apace.
But the sound wasn't sad,
Why, the sound sounded merry.
It couldn't be so,
But it was merry. Very.

And the editor with wrinkles furrowing his skull
Stood puzzling and puzzling, "They're not upset at all."
"They're correcting their spellings. They're checking the
    dash.
They're looking up hyphens, commas, and caps."
And he puzzled and puzzled till his puzzler was sore.

Then he thought of something that he hadn't before.
"Maybe analysts," he thought, "want to follow our style.
They're not all pig-headed. Just give them a while."

Well, what happened then?

In Langley, they say, that the editor's patience grew three
    sizes that day.
And now that he no longer felt like a jerk,
He called up his computer and checked on their work.
He proofread their copy, each one he did read
And he, the editor himself, signed off on their *SEIB*.

Delta Datas were among the first computers to grace the Agency's cube farms. They were eighty characters wide (the width of the classic IBM card) and monochrome. They didn't do Windows, or graphics, or much of anything else, but they did help get our job done. But they also were slow, and sometimes balked, inspiring this song:

Ode to the Delta Data
On, my Delta Data
I gotta tell ya how I hate ya
With your Beeping voice
"You've just been logged off"
User-hating controls
Try 'em and the screen rolls
Parallel, this format?
I just scoff.

When you try to call up
The toneless voice says "full up"
Try again *mas tarde*
If you dare
Working here in L.A.
I'm typing damn near all day
It's at the C.R.T. that
I must stare.

When the system goes down
I sit. It's like my job's blown
So dependent am I on this
Chunk of wire
Frustration in me growing
I think I'm close to blowing
To destroy this thing
Is my one desire.

To them in the Army I plea
Have you something there for me?
That I might rid myself of my
Nemesis?
Old Bill cuts loose a smile
And ruminates a while
Before he says "what you need
Is this."

It's back to work that I go
Wary eye on the SPO
Lest he note that
I've beneath my coat
I hustle into Peru
Intent on what I must do
Bits in the Potomac
They will float.

"What!?" you say I'm heartless
And in addition I'll be smart-less
Sans access to the AIM
Or MDS
I pause for one long moment
And let the idea foment
And consider: what result,
This mess?

By God, I think that you're right
I've been much too uptight
It's time that I made friends
With this machine.
I to the keyboard settle
Intent to test my mettle

My eagerness for détente
Honed keen.

To logon it refuses
And from my hair down to my shoe-ses
I feel a surge of fury
Course my veins
But sanity still grips me
I'll not have anger gyp me
I teeter, but pull quickly
Back the reins.

I call up Witching Center
And bid the data enter
And Lo, behold, the characters
Appear.
The logon I do finish
Without hairpulls or a grimace
It would appear for once the coast
Is clear.

The upper echelons have asked
If I'd mind being tasked
With a triple-digit
Paged report
Mind? Hell, I'd be grateful
My filing, I've a crateful
And my only other project
Hit "Abort."

To project I lunged full cry
And typed 'til I must near died
A masterpiece was spun from my

Hard toil.
Throughout this mighty odyssey
My Delta Data toiled with me
Détente had made a friend of
My once-foil.

Through trial, bonding occurred
And despite what you may have heard
There actually is something to
That stuff.
We digested stacks of tomes
And ignored our happy homes
We hung together as the going
Became tough.

With project fin'ly completed
I felt that I'd defeated
The animosity that'd fed
Upon my soul.
'cause that former terror
Had, *without one error*
Accepted every keystroke
Without toll.

Joyful, happy, contrite,
To have fought and won the good fight
My fingers reached to type in the
Last word
And as P-R-I-N-T
Went to machine from me
A discordant beep made its
Presence heard.

A nanosecond followed
In which my heart went hollow
And adrenal glands excitedly
Behaved.
Then, worst fears confirmed
Nightmare real as I learned
The message was succinct:
"No text saved."

Shock, betrayal, and confusion
As my brain went into fusion.
One last coherent thought
The mind retained:
The detonation sequence for
The 20 ki's of fresh C-4
I'd formed into a desk
And walnut stained.

The blasting cap bore stencil
Reading "number two lead pencil"
And my black line was the trigg'ring
Circuit trip.
I rigged it all to fire
And hooked up the last wire
Which'd been made to look just like a
Paper clip.

The havoc you can wreak
With just an ounce of good plastique.
Then imagine how the twenty
Ki's'll go.
I hit the fire alarm

So that none would come to harm
And the boys could gather outside for
The show.

Well it did the trick just fine,
Well done, Army mine.
It blew it all and left a
Happy glow.
The only problem was
As I came off my anger buzz
I was selling shoes
In Idaho.

A Tribute to the CIA's Office of Scientific and Weapons Research (OSWR) RIP: 1980-1995. (Sung to the tune of "American Pie" by Don McLean):

Long, long time ago
I can still remember how telemetry used to make me smile.
And I knew if I had my charter that I could make our
     weapons smarter
And maybe, we'd be happy for awhile.
But the Cold War made me shiver, with every Tebac I deliver
Star Wars on the door step, I couldn't take one more step.
I can't remember if I cried when I read we were to
     reorganize
And something touched me deep inside
The day the Office died.

Bye, bye OSWR
Hail Tsunami. Hail to AVAD. Hail to Kapunstinyar.
And good ol' boys were drinking beer at the bar;
Singing this will be the day that I die,

This will be the day that I die.

Did you write the Chart of Org and did you brief the
    Corporate Board?
If the EXDIR tells you so.
Now do you believe in rock and roll?
Can proliferation save your mortal soul?
And can you teach me the Third World, real slow?
Well, I know you've partnered with CPD
'Cause I saw you meeting in 5P
You both pulled off a coup,
And I dig those reports of blue—ooh!
I was a lonely senior analyst
With a typescript balled up in my fist
But I need a new dissem list
The day the Office died.

Now for four months we're OWTP
The jokes are flying fast and free.
But that's now how it used to be.
Then the Lotus Note came from Tom and Chris
C'mon, name the office, take a risk.
And the votes then came from you and me.
Oh, and while the Director was looking down
The Divisions moved their chairs around.
The meeting was adjourned.
No phone calls were returned.
And while Lenin read a book of Marx
The Soviets kept us in the dark.
And we guessed their strength on a lark
The day the Office died.

Helter skelter, in a summer swelter.

NBCD is off to a fallout shelter
Churning out IMs really fast.
WMD on the grass
NPC had an action to pass
But the staffer in the briefing didn't ask.
The Soviets made weapons by the score
While the contractors charged more and more
We were glad to pay.
Thought we'd never see the day.
MPD tried to take the field.
The CASD folks refused to yield.
Do you recall what was the feel
That day the Office died?

Oh, and there we were in one place
SSD is lost in space.
With no time left to start again.
So, c'mon, draft a paper, just be quick,
Coordinate until you're sick.
'Cause footnotes are the Office's only friend.
Oh, as I explained a missile stage,
My hands were clenched in fists of rage.
No RP born in hell
Cold break that SOVA spell.
And as the flames climbed high into the night
To light the propellant right,
I saw DIA laughing with delight
The day the Office died.

I meet a DDI who sang the blues.
And I asked him for some happy news.
But he just smiled and turned away.
I went down to the radar store

Where I saw the telemetry years before
But the man there said the FIS tape wouldn't play.
And in the halls, the IAs screamed.
The analysts cried and the Branch Chiefs dreamed
But not a word was spoken.
The CSP system was broken.
And the Communists I admire most,
Gorby, Yeltsin, and Khrushchev's Ghost
They caught the last train for the coast
The day the Office died.

In addition to farewells to offices that are reorganized out of existence,
farewells are frequently given to departing colleagues. These ceremonies
often showcase the lyrical and poetic abilities of those who remain. One
office celebrated the quirks of its ugly-necktie-wearing, limerick-spouting,
pentatonic-chime-playing branch chief by hosting a limerick and poem
contest:

There once was a poet named Ed
Who drew laughter at all that he said
His limericks were wild
Guaranteed that you smiled
And were much better heard than read

Ed once had a branch in PPAG
Where the dress code was really a drag.
If you wanted to advance
And leave nothing to chance
Wear a tie that'd make GQ gag.

His ties were a riot, really a blast:

Once your eyes focused, they stayed glued fast.
If ties are the mirrors of the soul
The outward signs of your self-control
What on earth does this tell us about Ed's past?

There was a smart fellow named Ed
Who wore ties every night to his bed
The chimes he did play
When he had a bad day
And the chime sounds just won't go away.

As branches go, WPB's been just great
A personality mix you could not re-create
Never up tight,
Serious but light
I'll cheer you ever onward—from outside the gate.

When I first joined this office
I couldn't help but notice
That management, though casual
And, dare I say, sometime unusual
Brought about an aura of comfort
Topped only by a constant effort
To see that all in their own way
Could demonstrate their ability
Need I say I will miss you all
But not worry after all
There will always be room for a visitor
And Paris is not bad with a translator

There once was a gal from Rhode Island
Who played diplomat in Ecuador's highlands
But she took a right turn
And diplomacy spurned
For the CIA's Mom, Country, and Apple Pie land
For intelligence sake
Her vows she did break
And abandoned her diplo career
In the greatest of games
She learned some small fame
As a nation to safety she steered
Now the game is all finished
And the Commies unbuckled
But her friends, foes and assets
Her bosses with blown gaskets
She will always remember
With a chuckle.

Admiral Stansfield Turner had his detractors while he served as DCI. In November 1977, the following song parody of Gilbert and Sullivan's work circulated in Headquarters. "Hank" in the poem is Enno Henry Knoche, deputy to former DCI George Bush; Knoche was fired by Turner after four months in office.

Of intelligence I had so little grip
That they offered me the Directorship.
With my brass-bound head of oak so stout,
I don't have to know what it's all about.

CHORUS: When he knows a whole ship from A to Z,
He surely can con the Agency
I know a man o'war from a bumboat raft,

But what kind of ship is called a trade-craft?
I never sailed a KUBARK, or spliced a PRQ,
And what's an esti-mate, I never had a clue.

CHORUS: He's stayed quite clueless so successfully
That he remains Director of the Agency.
If anyone objects, I'll have him walk the plank;
If you don't think I mean it, just ask good old Hank.
I may run the ship aground if I keep on so,
But I don't care a fig; I'll be the CNO.

CHORUS: He'll be the CNO, so thinks he.
So why give a fig for the Agency?

DCI Humor

Humor reaches to the "highest levels of the Agency," including the office of the Director of Central Intelligence, as seen in the following stories.

The first days of the first DCI, Rear Admiral Sidney Souers, were tough. A former OSS officer asked him what he wanted to do. Souers replied, "I want to go home."

Things were no easier for DCI General Walter Bedell Smith. On August 23, 1950, he wrote to Assistant Secretary of State for UN Affairs John D. Hickerson regarding his nomination, "I expect the worst and I am sure I won't be disappointed." He later told a senior FBI officer, "I'm afraid I'm accepting a poisoned chalice."

DCI Allen Dulles recalls a Soviet propaganda roundup by Ilya Ehrenburg in Izvestiya, who suggested that if Dulles ever made it to Heaven, "he would be found mining the clouds, shooting the stars, and slaughtering the angels." Dulles often used this job description in his public addresses when called upon to explain the duties of the Director of Central Intelligence.

When I left the Agency after the Bay of Pigs, DCI Allen Dulles said he would be happy to see me before I left, if I wanted to drop by. Of course I said I would. We had a nice chat at the end of which I asked him if he minded my asking a personal question. He said go ahead. I told him I had always smoked a pipe and knew that he did, too. I asked him why. He said; "You know, in this business you have to go to lots of meetings. I find that smoking a pipe is very helpful. When something comes up that I don't know the answer to, I just puff on the pipe, look wise, and let the guy next to me reply."

DCI Dulles was testifying before the Senate Armed Services Committee in the early 1960s. Halfway through, a Senator asked a pointed question and the DCI leaned over to an aide, in earshot of the Senator, saying, "give me the red notebook." The aide replied that he didn't have one. Dulles told the Senator, "I'll have to get back to you on this one." In the limousine on the way back to Headquarters, he explained to the flustered aide that "there is no red notebook. But the answer bought us time for a better answer to the question."

DCI Vice Admiral William Raborn had a sterling career that included developing the Polaris submarine, among other things. But when he came to the Agency with no background in intelligence or international issues, he knew he was in deep waters. During briefings, Raborn would often stick to areas in which he knew something—matters naval—usually asking questions about the country of the daily briefing's navy, even for landlocked countries. At another briefing on Latin America, he stopped the briefer to observe, "That's all very well and good. But I hear that there's this Arab who runs things and you haven't mentioned him at all?" "Arab, sir? Can't say as there's anyone in charge of Arab extraction." "Well, son, I've heard about this Ali Garchy. Just who is he?"

DCI Raborn also invited his senior staff and their wives to his home for a morning brunch. The conversations were a bit uncomfortable due to the cultural/background gulfs between them. At one point, someone noted a European automaton bird in a cage that graced the dining room. This became the topic of conversation for the rest of the meal before everyone was able to excuse themselves because of the press of business.

In a coordination meeting for a National Intelligence Estimate, there was a technical discussion by Intelligence Community security chiefs regarding what appeared to be advanced security procedures around a Russian site. DCI Raborn asked if it was simply regular anti-aircraft emplacements. DDS&T Albert "Bud" Wheelon replied that it would be like cracking walnuts with an elevator.

Before becoming DCI, James Schlesinger served as Chairman of the Atomic Energy Commission. An underground nuclear explosion was scheduled for Alaska. A Representative from Hawaii feared that a resultant tsunami would swamp Hawaii and that radiation would cause sterility, illnesses, and other vaguely-described and little-understood unpleasantness. Schlesinger replied, "Don't worry. I'll take my family up there to prove everything is safe." Soon after, or so the story goes, he became DCI and his new secretary reportedly handed him a note, saying, "The good news is you're not sterile. The bad news is, I'm pregnant."

DCI William Casey was known for his intellectual curiosity about science and technology. He would enjoy conversations with members of his staff on a variety of scientific matters. He was especially interested in interacting with the Science and Technology

Advisory Panel (STAP), a group of outstanding scientists, who met periodically to advise him on various matters related to the analysis of foreign science and technology.

When a new chairman of STAP was selected, Casey wanted to meet with him for a discussion. The meeting took place in the DCI's office and was a very lively one that Casey seemed to be enjoying very much. At one point he asked the chairman, who was an internationally known scientist, about a special project at the Pentagon that he had heard something about. The chairman, with as much tact as possible, said that he had checked that morning and found that Casey did not have the clearance necessary for him to discuss it. After the DCI hit the ceiling and returned to his chair, he shouted to his executive assistant, "Get 'Cap' on the phone immediately." After a short delay, a heated conversation ensued at the end of which Secretary of Defense Caspar Weinberger asked to speak to the scientist, who was told it was okay to discuss the project with Casey. At that point I was excused from the room and the two continued the discussion. I still don't know what the project was.

I am confident that if Secretary Weinberger had said "no" to Mr. Casey, the next call would surely have been to Ronald Reagan. Knowing the right people makes a big difference.

DCI William Casey's frequently unintelligible mumbling was legendary in the Agency's hallways, on the Hill, and within the media. He was often called the only man in government who didn't need a secure telephone.

One day, when the DCI was testifying before a Congressional committee, he was asked to comment on an article on the CIA that had run in *Playboy*. He had not seen it, and said that he'd get back to the committee. The Main Library did not have a copy, but because it was for the Director, the librarians, all of them very embarrassed women, scoured the local barbershops and bars for a fugitive copy, and finally located one, to the entertainment of the local barflies. Vowing never to face this gauntlet again, they put in subscriptions for *Playboy, Penthouse, Viva, Oui,* and just for balance, *Playgirl.* The current copies were kept in a safe behind the reference desk, known only to those with a very distinctive need-to-know. I learned about this when I was digging through the terrorism files, which were in a back room, and heard a "heh, heh, heh" emanating from the stack next to mine. Lo and behold, my colleague had found the file of back issues of these, *um,* research journals.

Former President and DCI George H. W. Bush was a frequent and popular guest at Headquarters. At the fiftieth anniversary of the founding of the Agency, President Bush addressed Agency employees, family members, and alumni, recalling, "After I left CIA . . . I was unemployed . . . And I was approached by the chairman of one of the largest corporations in America. 'We would like you to be on a Board of Directors, sir,' he said. Well, it interested me. And then there was a long, deathly silence. Nothing. Didn't hear from him. And then in comes a message. 'Well, our CEO and our Board feel that since you worked at CIA, maybe it wouldn't be good for you to come join our prestigious company.' The company went bankrupt a few years later, and I became President of the United States."

When a colleague of mine received the Distinguished Intelligence Medal about twenty years ago, I was invited to attend the ceremony in the DCI's conference room. Such ceremonies were always impressive but normally took place on a rather precise time schedule. The audience would gather, then the DCI would enter the room at 11:30 am. In this case he did not arrive at that time and soon it was 11:35, 11:40, and then 11:45. The audience became a bit restless and wondered what was wrong. At about that time, the door to the inner office opened and in walked two glamorous girls dressed in country music costume, including boots, short skirts, and cowboy hats. They were followed immediately by the DCI, Judge William Webster. He politely introduced Naomi and Wynonna Judd, the well-known mother-and-daughter singing duo, to the startled audience and the ceremony proceeded normally, except that more eyes were on the Judds than on the DCI and recipient of the medal.

It seems that the Judge had met the Judds at a social function and during casual conversation had suggested that they come to Headquarters for a visit the next time they were in town. With no announcement whatsoever, they arrived at the guard gate and asked to see Judge Webster. The startled guards could hardly believe their eyes but got in touch with the DCI's office and the Judge, a perfect gentleman, could do nothing but invite them to come in. After a short visit in his office, the three joined the awards ceremony that will not be forgotten soon by those who were present. It was a bit different.

DCI William Colby told my graduating Career Trainee class that the most effective operations officer is not a flamboyant James Bond type, but rather the quiet individual who blends into the environment, and can't even catch the eye of a waiter. I must have been pretty good at this, because I can't even get served in the drive-up line at McDonald's.

During the early and mid-1980s, I was a member of a branch in Geography Division. We shared a vault with the brand new Counter Terrorism Center. DCI Bob Gates came in and asked our secretary to take him to the C/CTC.

Carol said, "May I see your badge, please?"

Bob said, "Yes." Took it out of his pocket and clipped it to his jacket.

Carol then said, "Come this way, please." and took him to see the C/CTC.

A short time later, she was summoned to see our office director Dave Cohen, we presumed for a bit of counseling. Just before she was to go in, one of Bob's aides popped in and asked Dave to present Carol with an autographed photo. The inscription read,

> To Carol,
> The most security conscious person in the building.
> With thanks,
> Bob Gates

DCI Gates, fresh from a European TDY, brought to his next staff meeting a box of Belgian chocolates, encouraging his staff to try one. The confections had been glued to the bottom of the box. Gotcha!

The following is an aphorism from Secretary of Defense Robert Gates, recalling lessons learned as Director of Central Intelligence, "in the intelligence business, when you smell the flowers, look around for the coffin." Gates, speaking at the military retirement of Admiral Michael V. Hayden, who was also serving as Director of the Central Intelligence Agency, on June 20, 2008, credited Hayden with frequently going down to the employee cafeteria, where "he looks for an empty seat, not an empty table. He once sat down at what turned out to be a baby shower. He offered a few potential names before he took his leave."

DCI R. James Woolsey did not have a close relationship with President Clinton. The story has it that they had not met before President Clinton announced that Woolsey would become the next DCI (let this be a lesson to those of you who are job-hunting.

If you have a really strong resume, you don't need to ace the job interview!). The arms-length nature of the relationship continued through Woolsey's tenure, and he apparently never met one-on-one with the President. One day, a nut crashed a Cessna into the Rose Garden of the White House. Word around the Beltway was that it was actually Woolsey, trying to get into the Oval Office to see the President.

DCI Woolsey was dedicated to keeping the workforce informed, as reflected in his last official act. The editor of *What's News at CIA*, the internal newsletter, had given him an article to bless before it was published. Woolsey intended to fax it back to the editor with any changes after reading it in his car on the way to a farewell meeting with Rep. Larry Combest, head of the House Permanent Select Committee on Intelligence. Woolsey had a few changes to make, but the car's fax took early retirement that day. Ever dedicated to the mission, Woolsey sent the car back with just the article in the backseat. The news made the deadline, and got to the workforce in time.

One of DCI John Deutch's favorite stories was about the excellence of DDCI George Tenet. He recalls that during a meeting with important foreign dignitaries, Tenet temporarily cleared the room to have a very private, very secret word with the DCI. Once the door closed, Tenet told him, "Your fly is open!"

DCI George Tenet, famous for his unlit cigars, was thwarted from lighting them up in his office by a government-wide ban on smoking inside the building, as well as by Stephanie Glakas-Tenet, his ever-vigilant wife. But not to be stopped, Tenet would sneak onto the seventh floor's outdoor patio via his private office door, often taking the Director for Operations with him for contemplative smoke-filled walks past the seventh floor offices of their colleagues. On occasion, Tenet would stop in front of the office window of the Director for Intelligence, and make faces at him during meetings.

DCI Tenet was a huge fan of the basketball team of his alma mater, Georgetown University, attending nearly every home game. His love of basketball extended to the Agency, where he coached an Employee Activities Association team. He had the toughest defense in the league—composed of his security team, all of whom were armed. Tenet could often be seen dribbling a basketball down the hallways of the seventh floor. In the office of a senior associate, he fired off a chest pass, which the associate missed. The ball crashed into the wall behind, and knocked down knickknacks in the adjoining office. He stayed with bounce passes after that.

DCI Tenet's Deputy Director of Central Intelligence, John McLaughlin, was a noted magician, often entertaining senior visitors with his sleight of hand. After dinner, McLaughlin turned a 1-peso note into a 1,000-peso note for Argentine President Carlos Menem. Menem later sent Tenet a note asking for McLaughlin to be seconded to his government as his Minister of Finance, who could single-handedly fix the government's deficit. McLaughlin was never at a loss for a magic trick. When I was escorting Danny Aykroyd down the seventh floor for a visit with the Deputy Director for Intelligence (Aykroyd was developing a TV series on the Agency, and intended to portray the DDI), McLaughlin wowed him with a card trick he always carried in his pocket. McLaughlin routinely delighted Agency children on Family Day by picking Agency challenge coins from behind the ears of our next generation.

DCIA Michael Hayden quoted then-DIA Director James Clapper as counseling, "There are only two kinds of activities that America's military undertakes. There are operational successes and there are intelligence failures."

DCIA Michael Hayden, on the occasion of his retirement from the Air Force, said "Now, at this point in my remarks I can stop using past tense and start using present and future tense, because CIA takes over paying my salary on the first of July. A big question is whether the workforce will still respect me when they see my selection of suits."

Several individuals have been nominated as DCI, but for various reasons, withdrew from the Senate confirmation process or otherwise did not make it through this gauntlet. When Ted Sorensen, President Kennedy's speechwriter, withdrew, the DCI Portrait Gallery in the Original Headquarters Building was very briefly graced with a hand-drawn sketch of him on lined paper, taped next to the most recent portrait.

The Hunt for Red October: The Untold Story

Editor's Note: When I was putting this book together, the number one suggestion of my colleagues was to get a copy of this near-legendary spoof on how the CIA's Directorate of Intelligence would cover the events described in Tom Clancy's Hunt. *Episodes of The Untold Story showed up at various coffeepot areas throughout the DI during the height of Clancy's popularity. (Clancy's* The Hunt for Red October *was released in 1984 and was made into a film in 1990). Its arrival was always eagerly awaited and passed around to the cognoscenti. I've maintained its episodic quality, adding chapter numbers that did not appear in the original. The spoof appears in its entirety.*

Introduction

A recent best-seller—made into a box-office hit—describes the adventures of a CIA analyst caught up in a whirlwind of danger and excitement as events of cataclysmic importance unfold before his eyes. While the novel has intrigued and entertained millions of readers, ~~few have even suspected that there is a core of truth in this otherwise fantastic account.~~ Only the loyal cadre of CIA analysts— locked in silence by a legally-binding contract—know the real story, a story more frightening than any work of fiction ~~could ever convey.~~ Now, the truth is revealed.

Warning: Any resemblance to persons living and working in

the CIA is no accident. Everyone should expect to find a little of themselves—and a lot of everyone else—in this story.

Episode One

The year was 1984, a time of stagnation in the Soviet Union, and of comfortable routine in the CIA's Office of Soviet Affairs (OSA). It began as the most ordinary of days. Jack Ryan, intrepid CIA analyst, strode into work after a brisk twenty minute walk in from the parking lot. In fact, Jack had been able to do without his evening jog since the parking situation had tightened and he found he was getting his aerobic exercise walking in from the Kamchatka zone of the Agency lot. Jack liked that: it was efficient.

Jack didn't actually need to work at the CIA: he was independently wealthy, or had been until he got the Fairfax County personal property tax bill on his new Trans AM. Mostly, Jack liked the highly charged atmosphere of short deadlines and constant surprises. He found the frequent coordination battles a healthy outlet for his aggressions; otherwise, he might have found himself hollering at his wife and kids and kicking the family Lab. Instead, he hollered at other analysts and kicked the laser printer.

This morning—a very ordinary morning—Jack grabbed a cup of coffee and headed for his computer terminal to read his morning mail. That was another thing he liked about the CIA—tens of millions of dollars worth of top-of-the-line computer equipment to back up the analytical efforts of the Agency's crack intelligence officers. Jack quickly paged through the traffic that had come in during the night. Suddenly he froze, his eyes fixed on the screen.

Episode Two

Yes, it was a very ordinary day at the CIA—the system was down, and Jack turned off his terminal and went off in hunt of a doughnut and the latest rumors on the pending reorganization. He returned, sated with pastry and gossip, to sort through the findings from his mail box. Suddenly a tidbit of intelligence caught his attention. According to an allied intelligence service, the prototype of the new "Oktyabr" class submarine had been launched a week early. The prototype, predictably enough, was called "Red October." "For once I'd like to see them call a vessel the 'Trotskiy,'" Jack snortled to himself, "or the 'Academician Sakharov!' That'll be the day." He got an extra loud guffaw out of that one. Jack prided himself on his keen understanding of the Soviet bureaucratic soul.

Even more intriguing was the picture and analysis which accompanied the news of the launch. The new submarine, photographed while still in dry dock, appeared to have a strange pattern on the side formed of two large black circles—almost like the ears on a Mickey Mouse cap, to Jack's mind. British intelligence speculated that these portals were part of a sophisticated new submarine propulsion system. The portals allowed water to flow into the sub to the propeller—an impeller in this case. It was located inside the sub, masking the sound of the bubbles, which provided the characteristic submarine signature. Such a sub would be almost impossible to detect with existing technology.

The implications were mind-boggling. A new generation of Soviet submarines, undetectable and loaded to the gills with ballistic missiles. This would undoubtedly upset the balance of forces between the superpowers and destabilize the existing world situation. Jack knew that the U.S. had nothing similar in the works for its own submarines—it would be years before the Navy could catch up with the Soviet technical lead. In the meantime, the Soviet submarine fleet could strike the U.S. mainland at will, undermining the guarantees provided by the MAD doctrine—that no superpower would launch a first strike against the other for fear of retaliation. Now, a massive and undetectable Soviet first-strike was well within the realm of the imagination. Clearly, this should be written up—the fate of the free world depended on it.

Episode Three

Perhaps more important, Jack's career depended on it. His paper, *The Evolution of Soviet Submarine Cadre Policy: Problems and Prospects,* had been in review for quite a while and was unlikely to see the light of day any time soon. Originally, this had been a fast-track project meant to hit the streets quickly. Jack was given one month to research and one month to draft. That was three years ago, and now he was no longer sure what exactly the paper said, and he cared less. In the meantime, what with redrafting, adding, subtracting, recasting, refocusing, highlighting, and toning down, he hadn't actually gotten anything else out. Anything. For three years. Jack needed this piece badly.

He burst into the office of Edgar Platonoff, his branch chief, afire with enthusiasm for the intelligence mission for the first time in three years. As he explained the significance of the launch of the "Red October" to Ed, visions of spin-offs danced through his head. Congressional briefings, surely a briefing at the NSC and the Joint Chiefs, perhaps the Coast Guard and even the President! Then there were the foreign travel possibilities—briefings in every NATO country, then on to other allied intelligence services, from Mexico to Vanuatu. And maybe—a Stakhanovite award.

Ed burst his bubble. "Just how far along are you on that article? It's due on Friday—you have three days left."

The article. "The New Soviet Naval Uniform: Costing the Burden." Jack hadn't made much progress in costing the burden, but he had a pretty good idea that there wasn't one. In fact, the only real reason for writing the piece was that Leo Hawkins, his group chief, had been intrigued by the color photos in *Tyl I snabzhenie* (a journal first) and requested the piece. He kept asking about its progress. Jack would mumble something about methodology and regressions, and that usually scared Leo away for the time being.

Ed wasn't so easy to scare, though. He knew what a regression was and had begun to suspect that Jack didn't. Jack decided to go for the direct approach: "Listen, Ed, this is a hot intelligence issue, a heck of a lot more important than the new naval uniform. We ought to get something out today. If we don't, DIA will get a hold of this, and . . . " Jack gave Ed a moment to absorb the implications of that possibility.

Ed was momentarily stricken by the thought of what DIA might do with the information, but not long enough to save Jack. "I want to see that draft on Friday. Then we'll talk about some kind of note on this."

Jack left Ed's office shaken. The fate of the free world was in his hands, and it looked like he'd end up dropping the ball.

Episode Four

Jack was halfheartedly attempting to cost brass buttons when Ed stuck his head in the door. "Listen, if you want, you can put together a one-liner on the 'Red October' business." Without waiting for an answer, he headed off, probably to initiate a priority reorganization of the branch mailboxes.

The brass button calculations disappeared unnoticed under a three month stack of *Krasnaya Zvezdas* as Jack rushed to draft his piece. Fortunately, the Agency had invested considerable resources in designing an application that would expedite the drafting and formatting of production. He logged onto the system and entered the program.

Two hours later, it was ready. It had required the assistance of two branch secretaries and the division and group secretaries augmented by a series of calls to sundry ADP experts, but the piece was finally formatted in proper Agency style. It contained only twenty words, but each was heavy with meaning:

Early launch of Soviet "Red October" prototype submarine . . . equipped with undetectable drive system . . . success could destabilize world balance of power.

After a quick branch edit in which the world "launch" was

changed to "trial," Jack got the change entered in only half an hour. He slipped the draft into his division chief's priority in-box and waited for the response.

Episode Five

Jack was estimating how much braid went into a lieutenant's dress uniform, multiplied by the number of lieutenants in the Soviet Navy, aggregated with other data using a Soviet wholesale price found in a 1955 issue of *Turkmenskaya Iskra,* and adjusted for the annual replacement cost based on an estimate of wear and tear at official functions. His office mate pointed out that a different braid design was used on the dress uniforms of submarine officers. Jack groaned and started over.

Suddenly Hal Judevine, his division chief, came in. In a grim voice, he ordered Jack to meet him in his office. Jack panicked. "He wants to know about the article," he thought, mentally reviewing everything he knew about ribbon costs in the Black Sea fleet as he followed Hal. The door closed behind him.

"Jack, I read your piece." Hal continued in a slow and parental tone: "You know, this is very important. I don't know if you're aware of this, but the Soviet Navy is conducting naval exercises in the North Atlantic. We knew that they were planning something of the sort, but we weren't expecting them in that particular location. We certainly weren't expecting anything this extensive: it appears that several fleets are involved. It looks like they may be monitoring the 'Red October' launch. Gail Schmidt is doing a note on the exercises; I want you to do a joint piece on this."

Jack was feeling mighty pleased. At last, someone grasped the importance of the "Red October." He decided to press his luck. "What about the article? I'm supposed to have a draft on uniform costs in on Friday."

"Of course I expect you to finish that as well. Also, I want to focus this piece on the technical end of things. Details on the new drive system. Cut the part about threatening the balance of forces between the superpowers." He leaned back in his chair and turned avuncular: "Jack, when you've been in this Directorate longer, you'll learn that you can't make these kinds of wild statements. Stick to the facts, the nuts and bolts of the issue."

Jack should have expected this. Hal's background was technical, and he was still weak on the larger concepts—and he knew it. What was worse, he suspected that others knew it, and had adopted an all-knowing air to mask his insecurity. He liked to focus pieces on technical issues because this allowed him to keep the upper hand. Still, Jack was surprised that a man of Hal's uninhibited ambition would take the chance of allowing such a hot issue to slip away.

Hal's voice interrupted Jack's character analysis. "By the way, Jack, I want this to go as a Special Analysis. Talk to Gail. I've already given her some notes on what I want."

"But doesn't the office already have forty Special Analyses in queue with the production staff? Maybe if we did it as a Note, it might get in more quickly," Jack pointed out, trying not to sound as if he were pleading.

"I know what I'm doing here!" snapped Hal. He picked up his scissors and began editing a paper, effectively closing the conversation.

Jack closed the door behind him, sick with disappointment and dread. By the time the piece ran, the Soviets would probably have a whole fleet of "Oktyabr'" class subs—headed straight for the US coast.

Episode Six

Jack headed off to face Gail Schmidt. "Genghis" Schmidt. Of course, Jack never called her that to her face. No one did. Still, the name fit, and no one ever thought of her as anything else. Jack had run afoul of Genghis before, and he still winced at the memories. The last time, three days of work on his part had been quietly absorbed into an article of hers—unacknowledged. This time, Jack was determined that he would defend himself.

As it turned out, there was very little for either of them to do. Hal's "notes" looked an awful lot like a rough draft. Jack's one sentence on the "Red October" had turned into a paragraph forested with words like "impeller," "hydraulic," and "cavitation." No one but an engineer would have guessed that the "October" represented an entirely new generation of Soviet sub. Jack quickly made one editorial change: he added his name as co-author. Genghis looked sullen, but let it stand.

Jack was emboldened. "I think we could strengthen the piece if we highlighted the fact that the new drive system makes the 'Red October' undetectable by U.S. ships. Maybe add some language about the Soviets gaining a technical edge."

Genghis responded like a shark that's smelled blood. "I believe Hal's instincts about emphasizing the technical aspects are sound. And as a senior GS-13, I consider myself the lead author on this. Jack, when you've been in this Directorate longer, you'll learn that management is usually right about these things." Genghis obviously wanted to get into management badly—she was already practicing. Jack—a very senior GS-9—gave up.

Hal was pleased with the draft. "This is an exceptionally fine piece. And do you know why it's so good? Because you followed my guidelines." Genghis beamed and smoldered—no mean feat, but then, she was a senior thirteen. Jack just played with his key chain.

Back at his desk, Jack waited for coordination comments. He didn't expect that anyone would have much problem with the piece. In its present form it was probably unintelligible to 99% of the analyst in the CIA, and to 100% of Washington's policymakers. Suddenly a shadow fell across his desk. As Jack looked up, he was filled with a sense of doom.

Episode Seven

It was the Experts. Actually only one expert, but after Sandra

Scavelli's visit to a poultry feather processing plant in Chita, a local paper had mistakenly referred to the visit of several US experts. The name seemed to fit. After all, she was the only analyst in the Office of Technical Research (OTR) who could do the monthly crossword puzzle in *Tyl I snabzhenie:* no one else knew the Russian equivalents for all the mechanical parts used on Soviet submarines. After twenty years with the Agency, Sandra knew in excruciating detail the strengths and weaknesses of every sub the Soviets had ever launched, and she used this knowledge like a weapon. Now she loomed over him like an iceberg. Jack felt like the Titanic.

"I'm afraid I don't understand why OSA is writing this piece. This falls within OTR's purview," she announced in imperious tones.

Jack faced her manfully. "Management wanted me to write it." True—sort of.

She drew herself up. "Your management wouldn't realize that there are major problems with both the substance and the analysis in this piece." It was a challenge.

Jack decided to accept. "What exactly do you have problems with?" he asked, then winced as he realized that he had dangled a preposition. He was vulnerable.

The Experts ignored the preposition and went straight for the jugular. "Everything," she stated, and contemptuously tossed the draft on the desk.

She continued as slowly and surely as an icebreaker. "I don't know what sources you used, but someone has made a serious error. The Soviets have not developed an impeller drive system."

"Sandra, I'm afraid you're wrong on that," Jack thought he had the advantage at last. "According to this report from British intelligence—complete with pictures, I may add—the Soviets have an operable impeller system on the 'Red October.'"

Her answer was as rapid and as categorical as machine gun fire. "The British are wrong. Don't tell me you believe something just because it appeared in print somewhere? After all, one wouldn't accept something as true simply because it appeared in a *Reuter* press release," she added.

Actually, Jack would. It had never occurred to him before that something printed in black and white might not be true. Jack felt his intellectual world begin to crumble around him as he contemplated that possibility—so he ignored it, and concentrated on the matter at hand. "Listen, Sandra, if the Sovs don't have an impeller drive system, what are those round black circles on the side of the 'Red October'?"

"Mickey Mouse ears. Someone has painted a Disney logo on the side of that submarine. We have already subjected these photographs to careful analysis using advanced computer models that analyze the light reflections from the various surfaces of the vessel—I would explore the details but you wouldn't understand."

Jack was getting mad. That was the stupidest analysis he had ever heard, and he was almost tempted to say so—but didn't. He was pretty sure, though, that Sandra was trying to snowball him with a lot of technical gibberish, and she apparently thought he was chump enough to fall for it. "We'll see about that," he thought to himself.

Out loud, he said, "Well, your comments are very thought-provoking, and we will certainly take them into account."

"I expect you to do so. I also expect that you will cancel any plans to run this piece." She turned to leave.

"Bitch!" Jack muttered softly, but not softly enough.

"Excuse me?" She turned back sharply.

"Rich, I said. Your comments are rich with substance." Jack hoped he had made a quick save.

"I see," she replied, and Jack was afraid she did.

Jack sank into despair. He was sitting on some of the hottest intelligence ever to come through the Agency, but it looked like one ego-mad engineer might be able to stop it from getting out—and changing the course of world history.

Episode Eight

Jack was searching his files for a wholesale price for seam binding when Rhonda Hoopingardner, the group secretary, entered to tell him that Leo wanted to go over the piece. He alerted Gail and they headed for Leo's office.

When they entered, they found Leo slumped over the note, a glazed look in his eyes. "Sit down," he said, "I have a few suggestions."

Jack sat down and made himself comfortable. He might as well— in his experience, a few suggestions usually took at least an hour.

"I'm a little disappointed in this draft," Leo began. "I thought every analyst understood the need to write simply and clearly. I know Gail writes well: I'm familiar with her work and this section on the naval exercises is very much to the point. Now, Jack, you'll develop a better feel for the Agency style in time. No policymaker is going to understand this technical terminology. I do, of course," he was quick to add, "but they won't."

Jack would have been very much surprised if a man who found it a challenge to open the vault in the morning understood a description of an impeller drive system, but he kept that thought to himself. Leo was a musicologist by training, and his efforts to handle the substantive aspects of his job evoked an image of a rubber dinghy in an Atlantic gale. Jack would have pitied the man if he hadn't been so dangerous.

"Now try to explain to me in layman's terms, Jack, just what this all means," Leo continued.

Jack quickly outlined the problems for sonar detection presented by the new propulsion system and the potential this innovation held for destabilizing the balance of forces between the superpowers. A look of relief spread over Leo's face. Something he could understand.

"Jack, this has got to run tonight. I won't permit any delays. Turn this into a note, and rewrite your section, and this time try to lean forward on the issue. Don't be afraid to write what you think."

Jack *was* afraid when he thought of Sandra Scavelli's likely reaction. Maybe he could satisfy her with a well-placed "according to one source" and "could be." The possibility was remote, but Jack had to try. He was now truly caught between the devil and the deep blue sea.

Episode Nine

It wasn't difficult to clean up the piece—Jack just used the language he'd originally had in mind when he proposed the piece. He raced a copy down to the front office and went to grab a bite in the cafeteria. Jack didn't particularly care for the cafeteria's food—it was overpriced and the quality was an unpredictable as the Soviet grain harvest—but with an eye surgeon for a wife, he could afford to eat $4 baked potatoes. Besides, eye surgery, errands, housework, and child rearing left Cathy Ryan with little time to make bologna sandwiches.

Jack fully intended to call Sandra Scavelli and try to negotiate some compromise language—as soon as he had fortified himself with the potato—but when he got to his desk he found a message to see the director of OSA. He quickly presented himself in Chris Deter's office. Deter motioned to him to take a seat. On the office director's desk Jack saw a sheaf of papers, covered with blue arrows as tangled as a Soviet fishing net. He was transfixed. It could be one of only two things: Jack's paper, or the plan for the office reorganization. He tried to get a closer look.

"Jack, I want this to run exactly as it is. I've just made one small change," Deter began.

Jack looked at the draft. This time, "trial" had been changed to "launch." This was too easy. He decided he'd better take his medicine like a man.

"Chris, we're having some problems with OTR. They don't believe the 'Red October' has an impeller drive system, and they want us to kill the piece."

"What's their explanation for the black circles on the side of the sub?" Deter looked at him intently.

"Mickey Mouse ears. They think it's a painted logo."

Deter burst out with the same guffaw that Jack had had to suppress when he first heard Sandra's analysis. "That's why OSA has the reputation of being the best office in the Directorate, and OTR doesn't. Listen, Jack, when you've been here longer, you'll learn that you can't allow coordination to reduce a strong, insightful piece to pabulum. Don't worry about OTR—I'll make sure they okay this upstairs."

Chris Deter might not be worried about OTR, but then he didn't have to face the Experts. Jack should have been prepared for this kind of reaction. Deter's predecessor, Jeff Brown, had been under inexorable pressure to increase current production. Richard Letizia, the head of the Directorate, was convinced that a steady parade of noteworthy events was taking place in Brezhnev's USSR, but that OSA apparently wasn't bothering to bring them to policymakers' attention. Brown's efforts to accommodate Letizia were reminiscent of a man overboard in Arctic waters. His last numb attempt was to send up a note on the Central Committee's changing attitude towards Rachmaninoff. Letizia's choice for the new Director of OSA had the vision Brown lacked—unhandicapped by any sense of perspective. Scuttlebutt had it he had requested a typescript on UFOs, and no intelligence product was too far out in left field if it made the Soviets look menacing. Still, in this case the threat was real—and more frightening than Deter could have hoped.

Episode Ten

Jack couldn't believe how quickly he had been swept along by the current of events. Just this morning he had been begging to write one sentence—now he was doing a top-priority note, and feeling a little queasy in the stomach. He told himself that it must be the pepperoni and cheese sauce from lunch, and tried to force from his mind images of a wrathful Sandra Scavelli by contemplating the possibilities of high-level briefings and career advancement. The new Soviet naval uniform slipped willingly from his thoughts.

Suddenly the ring of the phone interrupted his reverie. He reached for the open line. Nothing. He reached for the other phone, but too late. The call had been automatically transferred to the secretary's desk. He looked out his office door. As usual, Roxanne Conners was out to lunch—and this time, she wasn't at her desk, either. Jack assumed the call was from the editorial staff, and alerted Gail. The two of them headed up to the seventh floor.

Joanne Snetzger was the editor for their piece. She was pleasant and professional. And a looker. "I wonder if she knows how to make bologna sandwiches?" he thought wistfully, but a pang of guilt prodded him back to scanning the piece. Pretty routine changes— "launch" had been changed to "trial." Jack no longer remembered which word had been his original choice.

Suddenly Gail let out a bellow. "Calisthenics?!" she cried. "The word is 'exercises.'"

"'Calisthenics' and 'exercises' are synonyms," Joanne answered coolly. Jack admired the way she stood up to Genghis.

Genghis steamed ahead. "Surely even a layman with only a cursory knowledge of naval terminology would realize that 'naval calisthenics in the North Atlantic' is complete nonsense. Change it."

"You're taking a very narrow attitude towards language usage."

"Who are you, anyway? A political analyst, I'll bet." Gail inflicted the worst insult she knew. Jack was sickened. Surely the lovely Joanne couldn't be a political analyst. Genghis was going too far.

Joanne admitted that in her most recent incarnation she had followed the political affairs of West Africa. Jack was disenchanted. He knew more than he wanted to know about political analysts. They left dirty spoons by the coffee pot and were suspected of careless attitudes regarding vault security. Only rumors, but where there's smoke. . . . Still, it could have been worse. She could have been from the Office of Global Affairs.

Genghis demolished what was left of the lovely Joanne, and she and Jack headed back down to their vault. They found chaos. Deter had finally unveiled his scheme for reorganizing the office, and everyone had been taken by surprise. They had made the usual economist's mistake—they had assumed rationality. Jack sought out Ed to learn his own fate. What he discovered chilled him to the bone.

Episode Eleven

Jack's new branch chief was Sandra Scavelli: the Experts. And what's more, all production was now on hold until the new management had an opportunity to review it. That meant Jack's paper was held up again. He also found out that Sandra had already held his piece until tomorrow. Jack realized with a sick feeling that she had surely known about this when they had talked that morning. Jack was really regretting that "b—" word now.

The casualties were high. Ed Platonoff had spent too much time reorganizing the branch mailboxes and not enough kissing ass. Now he was headed for the Office of Training, rumor had it, to teach "Getting To Know Your Computer." Hal Judevine's technical expertise had scuttled one too many of Deter's creative forays into analysis and he was being suitably rewarded. He now held a highly visible and powerless job in the front office masterminding the office's ADP strategy. Leo Hawkins seemed to be the only winner. It was said that Deter and Hawkins were both opera aficionados and had season tickets for adjacent seats at the Kennedy Center. His musical background had stood him in good stead—he was now head of the political group, a more visible post, and one that would free him from any contact with regressions. Jack decided to pick up a Puccini tape on the way.

Home. It sure felt good after the day's madness. Cathy was going to be late—the kids' ballet lessons were today—so Jack headed for the fridge. He stared into its depths. He saw the bologna and the bread but didn't make the connection. Instead, he went for the frozen pizza, and spent the evening, as usual, working on his latest screenplay. Jack had achieved some success in writing scripts for horror films. Sometimes his writing presented a pleasant diversion from his work life. Sometimes he had trouble telling the two apart. This was one of those nights.

He slept fitfully. In his dreams, Hal Judevine took away his Delta Data and replaced it with a typewriter. He tried to protest, but Hal insisted he knew what he was doing. Jack woke up to find his finger tapping at the bedside table, a dream-inspired effort to find the Print key on the typewriter.

At work again, he managed to avoid Sandra and head for his terminal. It was still there. As he paged through his mail, something caught his eye. Something so startling that Jack almost spilled his coffee in excitement. The "Red October" launch was even more important than he had thought.

Episode Twelve

Jack slowly scrolled through the conversation of submarine warrant officer Faizullah Rakhimov and Captain Marko Ramius, savoring each word. It was three months old, but still thrillingly relevant:

1. *The following conversation between two officers in Qarshi, Uzbekistan and Murmansk illustrates the declining morale and discipline in the soviet officer corps. These two are evidently planning to go on a major shopping spree (Operation Sausage) in the first western port in which their ship docks, and intend to party hearty the rest of the voyage.*

2. *Qarshi: Captain Ramius? This is Mr. Rakhimov. (Govorit Michman Rakhimov.)*

3. *Murmansk: Yo Rakhimov! What's happening? (Nu kak dela, Rakhimov?)*

4. *Qarshi: My orders have come through as you requested. I'll be one of your officers on the "Red October." (Nfi)*

5. *Murmansk: Totally excellent! (Ochen' khorosho!) The others have*

also received their orders. Those fools (duraki) in Moscow actually trust me. Will they be in for a big surprise in a few months! Ha ha ha (kho kho kho)

6. *Qarshi: I can taste the hot dogs and cotton candy (sosiki i sladkuju vatu) already! Usa, here we come! (my plivjem v ssha!)*
7. *Murmansk: Hush! No one but our fellow officers must know about "operation sausage." (operatsija "kolbasa")*
8. *Qarshi: Right, catch you later—on the "Red October."*
   End of message

Perhaps no one else in the Intelligence Community understood the message's true meaning, but Jack did. He was glad now he'd spent three long years of his life on submarine cadre policy. He might be the only person in the free world who understood what was in Captain Ramius's mind—and its portent for the strategic balance of forces. He rushed to Sandra's office to save his piece—and the Western world.

Episode Thirteen

"Sandra," he began, "I've got to rewrite my piece completely."

"I'm glad you realize that. A wise decision—if a belated one," she said as she prepared to accept his obeisance.

"Listen, there's new information in." He ignored her jibe and continued. "I'd show you the text but the printer's down. It seems that the captain of the 'Red October' is Marko Ramius, their top submarine officer and a man expected to replace Gorshkov someday. I've discussed him thoroughly in my draft on submarine cadre policy." Jack knew she had read it—he recognized scraps of it on her desk next to the tape dispenser. "It now looks like Ramius intends to defect—with the 'October.'" Jack waited for the import of his words to sink in.

He waited in vain. "I read that report. It said that he was planning to go shopping."

"The report said he was planning to go shopping. You don't believe everything you see in print, do you?" He thought he was pretty clever.

The Experts thought he was simply insubordinate. "I suggest that you keep to the subject at hand and explain how a craving for cotton candy translates into a plan to defect."

"It's the only explanation that holds water. Ramius is the finest officer in the Soviet Navy, a man of impeccable integrity. Such a man would never abuse his position simply for a lark in a Western port. In fact, no Soviet submarine—and certainly not the 'October'— is going to dock in a Western port. The clue is in the phrase 'Operation Sausage.' You see, Ramius's wife died after eating a bad Soviet sausage. I believe that he and his crew are defecting as an act of protest against the Soviet Union and the disastrously low quality and variety of its consumer goods."

"The quality of Soviet sausage is certainly low," Sandra noted thoughtfully, her face a little pinched—she was undoubtedly remembering her own encounters with Soviet sausage in Chita. Then she snapped out of her reverie. "You'll need more evidence than that to convince me. I think you'll find that my standards for intelligence are a little higher than those to which you have been accustomed." There had never been any love lost between Ed and Sandra.

"Now, let's discuss the article you're writing on the share of the new naval uniform in the Soviet defense burden . . ." Jack settled in a chair, his stomach churning as if a fleet of Soviet sausages was cruising the waves there. It looked as if there was no escape.

Suddenly Genghis Schmidt burst in. "Sandra, I'm going to rewrite my piece." Jack noticed that it was now her piece. He bided his time.

"I'm sorry, Gail, but I simply don't believe that the 'Red October' is on a hunt for cotton candy. I've killed the piece."

"Cotton candy? Forget the 'Red October'—I think the Soviets

may be preparing for WWIII! These are more than naval exercises—the Sovs now have everything that floats heading towards the North Atlantic. They've even mobilized the 'Avrora'!" Gail was breathless.

"Gail, your analysis is unsubstantiated and logically flawed." It looked like Genghis had met her match. "There must be a more reasonable explanation for this fleet mobilization."

"There is!" Jack blurted out. "They must know that the 'Red October' is defecting and have ordered every seaworthy vessel they have to hunt it down and destroy it before it can enter U.S. waters."

"Whatever the explanation, given fleet activity on such a large scale, we have no choice but to write a piece for tomorrow's book." At last—Sandra was on board.

"I've already started drafting it," Genghis jumped in, eager to make up lost ground. Her nose for intelligence was both keen and brown. Jack felt marooned. It seemed the ship of current intelligence was sailing without him.

Episode Fourteen

Then, like a typhoon, Tim Greer stormed into the room. "I've read Jack and Gail's draft—this is incredible! We've got to get this out immediately! A high-priority note, follow it up with a typescript!" Jack was starting to feel better. Their new deputy division chief was the kind of guy who could see beyond the naval uniform costing effort.

Sandra filled Tim in on the new developments—with caveats. The new information was swept up in a tidal wave of enthusiasm, the caveats lost in the undertow. "Incredible! The biggest breakthrough in submarine technology in decades about to fall into US hands! Think of the repercussions—we'll be briefing this for years!" Tim had been in middle management as long as Jack could remember, watching as an assortment of the ruthless, the obsequious, and the hopeless were promoted above him. Apparently he was hoping this would be his chance to join the parade. Jack wondered which tack Tim was going to choose.

It didn't take long to draft a new version of the piece in accordance with Tim's guidelines. He told them to highlight the technical innovation embodied in the new sub, and the chance that the prototype might end up in the possession of the US Navy. Gail did venture to ask whether they should clear the decision with Murray Lisook, the man who had replaced Hal Judevine as division chief. "Not necessary! Murray and I have streamlined division procedures—he handles papers, I supervise current production. The new review process is going to go like greased lightning—trust me!" Jack had heard that phrase before—this time he thought he'd wait and see.

Sandra still thought it was safer to give Murray a drop copy. Safer for her career, perhaps—but not for national security, as they soon learned to their horror.

Episode Fifteen

Murray called them all into his office. He had some thoughts to impart on the subject of the "Red October."

Tim was obviously hot under the collar, no doubt anticipating that his big opportunity to schmooze with the Front Office was going to drift away. "Yo, Murray! I thought we'd agreed I'd handle review for current pieces—avoid double jeopardy at the division level. We were going to streamline the review process . . ."

"Now Greer, one more review session never did a piece any harm." Jack wondered if Murray had ever been an analyst.

Murray launched into his analysis of the developments in the North Atlantic. Jack remembered a description he had heard from a co-worker who had once been in Murray's branch. The analyst had commented that Murray's reviews could only be described using Russian indeterminate verbs: they were multi-directional, habitual, involved repeated motion, and often resulted in a round trip—Murray led the analysts all over the map, only to bring them both back where they started. This time was no exception.

"It seems to me," Murray began, "that maybe we're headed in the wrong direction here. Maybe the Soviets are planning to attack NATO."

"It is unlikely that the Soviets would choose to attack NATO's forces in the Atlantic where they are strongest. And surely they would begin an attack in a more subtle fashion." The Experts had spoken.

"Well, maybe this 'Red October' is manned by kamikaze Cold War fanatics who want to fire on the US and try to start WWIII." *Dr. Strangelove* had been on cable last night. It looked like Murray had been up past his bedtime.

"Given the range of the 'October's' missiles, it could have launched a strike from the Barents Sea. We would not be here to discuss this subject if its officers had planned to launch a first strike against the US." The Experts's words had acquired an Arctic chill.

"Now I just read this other report. There's a guy over there that says nuclear war is imminent." It was worse than Jack had thought. Murray had gotten a hold of a piece of raw intelligence.

"'That guy' is a blind Bulgarian soothsayer quoted by a babushka who'd met his mother while they were both standing in line for cabbage. I hardly need to say more."

Apparently she did. Murray looked as lost as a ship in a pea-soup fog. The Experts boomed out like a fog horn. "I'm afraid that since the source had no access and no reliability, this intelligence is worthless."

"Well, let me think about this. Hold on to this draft while I try to get a clear picture of what's happening here." That might take forever, Jack thought despairingly. In the meantime, the Soviet fleet was closing in on the "Red October."

Episode Sixteen

Jack had calculated without Tim Greer, who was not about to allow his big career opportunity to sink below the waves while

Murray gummed the piece to death. Instead, he had again chosen to indulge his penchant for "the Great Game," which he played as subtly as any nineteenth century British officer. Tim slipped an FYI copy into Tom Metzger's priority in-box.

Tim understood his quarry well. Their new group chief had risen up the ranks through a rapid series of career moves that never left him time to be an expert in any one area. He had only one field of real expertise—spotting a career opportunity and grabbing it. He knew what to do with this one.

Within minutes, Tom was closeted with Murray and Tim. Jack didn't know what had gone on, but he overheard scraps of their conversation as they concluded their meeting and exited Tom's office.

"This may be the hottest piece of intelligence in a lifetime," Tom was saying. "For a submarine captain to defect, and bring with him the prototype of a new generation of Soviet sub . . . dynamite!"

"My thoughts exactly," piped in Murray.

"Jack!" Tom called out as he spotted him at the coffee pot. "In the future, when you find out about something this important, I'd like you to alert me immediately. You'll learn in time that intelligence of this magnitude has to be moved along quickly."

Jack was sure grateful for the advice, but thought to himself that like manure, it might be of more value if it were spread around— maybe at the office staff meeting.

"Oh, and Jack? I'd like a copy of your paper to read right away. I'm going to be briefing this information around town this afternoon, and I'd like to be filled in on everything."

Jack was elated—at last, interest in his moribund draft—and from a man who obviously knew how to get things done. He scurried to get a copy of the paper. Easier said than done: the printer was down. He went to look for Sandra's copy. He came back with a burn bag and a sheaf of cuttings. He, Roxanne, and a roll of scotch tape eventually produced a readable copy. Within an hour, Tom and

Genghis were off to brief the President and an assortment of other policymaking luminaries. Jack was left to handle coordination—and to search for a wholesale price for shoelaces. Suddenly the phone rang.

Episode Seventeen

Jack picked up the receiver to hear a voice on the other end command: "My office. Now!" A click. Jack didn't need to ask who it was. It could only be Teddy Murphy, the Deputy Director of OSA. Chris Deter and Leo Hawkins had left that day for a three-week SIS-bonding mission in the Pacific—allegedly to check with all and sundry on the Soviet menace in the Pacific basin. Deter apparently believed that the Soviets presented the greatest threat in Fiji and Tahiti, since that was where they were scheduled to spend most of the trip. A stop in Australia was also planned—undoubtedly to check out Soviet penetration of the Sydney opera house.

Jack dutifully set off for Murphy's office. As he entered, OSA's deputy director was talking simultaneously on both phones while chewing out a hapless branch chief who'd wandered in at the wrong time. Eventually he disentangled himself from the phone lines, the branch chief found an opportune moment to escape, and Jack was left facing the office's best known—and oldest—legend.

"Son, I liked this," he began. "It looks like the food problem is worse than we'd thought—no wonder Brezhnev's worried. A few more faulty sausages and he could go the way of Khrushchev. Did you know the 'khrushch' means 'corn blight'? I'm sure that's significant."

Jack sat nervously. Perhaps he was supposed to comment on this.

Apparently not. Murphy continued. "Ryan, you don't remember those days, but people used to wait with bated breath for our national accounting estimate. People wanted to know what Soviet GNP was. Now they can't even spell it."

Jack waited for the submarine tie-in. Was he missing something?

"Now, Ryan, I hope you use oblast' handbooks. Robert Finkelstein won a cash award once for finding a 1962 production figure for zinc in the Irkutsky handbook. Changed the whole picture for non-ferrous metallurgy. Raised our GNP estimate by .01 percent. A real analyst, Finkelstein."

Maybe Jack should say something about titanium at this juncture. Or was Murphy leading up to the naval uniform costing effort?

"There's a fellow in another office who has a whole basement filled with oblast' handbooks. Had to get rid of the pool table, but who wouldn't?"

Jack gave up. He was completely lost. He practiced his silent but studious expression. He kept it on the ready for just such an occasion.

"I knew a case officer once who was sent to Burundi. He and his whole family had their appendixes out before they left. You should think about that, Ryan, in case you go to the Soviet Union."

Good Heavens! He was being sent on rotation!

"So as I was saying, I want a box on the Food Program. Implications for the succession struggle and Kremlin politics. With food developing as a key issue, maybe this ag honcho Gorbachev could move to the forefront."

This was getting silly. And time-consuming. Murphy began a rambling discourse on the value of high quality silage in improving livestock feeding efficiency. At this rate, Jack would never get his note up to the production staff on time. He was trapped!

Episode Eighteen

Then the phone rang. Murphy picked it up, and Jack was out the door before the Deputy Director could stop him. He was off to vault the next hurdle—he had to get an agriculture analyst to do a box on the Food Program and its implications for the succession struggle.

He wended his way to the isolated enclave where agriculture analysts were kept. Thank goodness—someone was there. It turned out to be Bill Henry. Bill had been with the Agency for thirty-five years. Some people thought he ought to have retired years ago. Others thought he already had. It looked like Jack was going to get the opportunity to form his own opinion on the subject.

Jack interrupted Bill's work on the *New York Times* crossword puzzle to explain the situation to him. The man looked confused. "So why are you coming to me?" he asked. "This sounds important."

Jack felt like he was trying to communicate with an extraterrestrial. "We need a box on the Food Program. ASAP. I was given the impression that you do agriculture."

"So they tell me," was Bill's offhand reply.

"So you must be familiar with the Brezhnev Food Program."

"Well, I've heard of it, of course. But it's not really part of my account. Mike Kayusa follows that. He covers the important stuff."

Jack had heard of Mike Kayusa. "Killer" Kayusa. Apparently Bill was one of his victims.

"So what exactly do you follow?" Jack was torn between pity and contempt for the man.

"All the stuff that isn't important. So if this is important, you'd better talk to Mike."

"So where can I find him?" Jack was somewhat relieved to be able to leave Bill to continue his retirement and to be able to turn to a more energetic analyst.

"He's on leave today." Jack prepared to start the siege again.

Suddenly the phones rang. Bill picked them both up and put one to each ear. He seemed to be an old hand at this. He hung them both up without having said a word and announced to Jack: "That was Murphy. I guess I'm writing a box on the Food Program." He paused for a moment, then wondered out loud: "I wonder if this means they'll put off the deadline for my project on costing the inputs for oilseed production?"

Suddenly Jack was struck by a sickening sense of recognition. Could this be Genghis and him twenty-five years from now?

Surely twenty-five years of bureaucracy mismanagement and bare-knuckled coordination battles wouldn't reduce intrepid Jack Ryan to this complaisant, hopeless lump of an analyst? Or would it? He decided not to try to answer that question. He'd remember the feeling, though, and work it into his next screenplay, *Horror at Bikini Beach*. Thank heavens he had a second career.

Jack set off for his desk, still shaken. The piece seemed more important than ever before. He rounded the corner, to find himself face to face with a new threat.

Episode Nineteen

It was the food processing analyst, bearing coordination comments. For someone who followed food for a living, Ann Oka was awful scrawny. But then Jack could see how reading about Soviet sausage production all day could make a person lose her appetite. Besides, he had the impression that she spent a good deal of her time writing comic literature for office entertainment. A definite light-weight. He prepared himself for another barrage of silly comments.

To his relief, she allowed as how Soviet sausage quality was rather low, and how a lot of Soviets were pretty put out about that. Thank goodness there were some universal truths in Soviet analysis. Jack suspected that Ann had also had personal experience with Soviet sausage. She wandered off, perhaps to write a poem about the quarterly results. Jack returned to his desk to do man's work.

The phone rang. He reached for the open line. Perhaps Cathy had finished surgery early and was home making a nice meal—Shrimp Creole, Chicken a la King? Jack had an active fantasy life. Nothing. He reached for the other phone, but too late. The call had been intercepted by another analyst. Once again, Jack assumed correctly that it was the editorial staff and headed up to read off on the piece.

This time he was alone with the lovely Joanne. He ogled her figure covertly and wondered what she looked like in an apron. Then he turned with a sigh to the job at hand—protecting his piece. Lost in a haze of culinary day dreams, he almost missed the slight editorial change. It was only one word, but it changed the whole meaning of the piece. But how to tell the lovely Joanne that she had made a catastrophic error? He decided to take the direct approach.

"Joanne, I'm afraid there's a world of difference between 'the prototype of an advanced submarine design' and 'the prototype of an advanced hoagie design.'"

"We try to keep the language we use as simple and nontechnical as possible. And submarine and hoagie are synonyms." She was confident and professional—but then so was Custer.

Jack plied her with details, drew sketches, tried every method of gentle persuasion he knew. Nothing. Finally he brought out the big guns.

"Joanne, if you don't change this word back to submarine, my division chief will come up here and scream and throw things. And then he'll get nasty." She backed down—and a good thing. Jack wasn't sure Murray knew the difference between a submarine vessel and a hoagie, either.

Jack felt he had won a Pyrrhic victory. He had lowered his standards as an analyst and a human being. And he'd lost all hopes of winning the respect and admiration of the lovely Joanne. He began to muse. What if she wasn't as dense as she seemed? What if she had guessed at his dreams and her use of the word "hoagie" was actually a subtle invitation? Now he'd never know. He could reassure himself that he'd accomplished his mission: his piece had run and had been picked up by another publication. The President had been alerted, and the free world was safe for the time being. But Jack knew the bittersweet taste of success. He went home that night a wiser man.

Episode Twenty

Jack was feeling considerably perkier the next morning when he set off for work. It looked like he'd escaped the naval uniform costing effort—a good thing, too; it had been due today. Interest in his masterpiece—the long dormant paper on submarine cadre policy—had revived. And he'd gotten out a successful note.

When he arrived at his desk he found a copy of *The Washington Post* on his chair. On the front page he recognized a picture of Captain Marko Ramius posed by the "Red October." Elated, he began reading the text. His elation soon faded. It seemed the "October" had arrived in a Florida port the night before. Ramius's first words on emerging from the submarine's hatch were: "I'm going to Disneyland!" When asked by the reporters what the significance of the black circles on the side of the submarine was, he explained that they were Mickey Mouse ears, painted by his crew as an act of defiance—and a guarantee that they would be unable to change their minds once they had undertaken their daring mission. According to the *Post*, captain and crew were now feasting on hot dogs and cotton candy.

Jack was in shock. The Experts had been right—there was no silent propulsion system on the "Red October." He'd made an idiot of himself in the eyes of all the office's management, weakened the Agency's credibility, and embarrassed his ambitious and ruthless group chief in front of the top policy makers in the United States government. And all this before he'd read his SAFE mail.

Sandra called him into her office. He decided to throw himself on her mercy.

"Sandra, you were right about the 'October.' I should have listened."

"I generally am right," she answered, but added grudgingly, "You were right about Ramius's desire to defect—and the reasons behind it. A nice bit of analysis."

Jack felt a little better. But not for long. She continued. "You still have a chance to redeem yourself. If you turn in a well-written piece on the contribution of the new naval uniform to the Soviet defense burden, we'll recommend you for promotion. You do have a draft ready, don't you? It's due today."

Jack inquired weakly, "What about my research paper? I should have a hard cover soon."

"I guess I should have told you right off. It's been killed. Tom felt that after all the high-level briefings he gave on the 'October' affair based primarily on your draft, it was no longer necessary to publish it. And it's a little out-of-date at this point."

Jack slunk back to his desk. It looked like his whole career would now depend on the naval uniform article. The phone rang. It was the production staff, calling to say the President had liked his piece on technical advances in Soviet sandwich design. Apparently they had run the wrong draft. Jack heard snickering on the other end of the line. Could it get any worse?

He began to search in his briefcase for an article he'd been reading on Soviet wholesale prices. He didn't find it, but he did find something else. A bologna sandwich. And a Twinkie. Cathy still cared! He purged his mind of all images of the lovely Joanne. Perhaps he had been unfair to Cathy. After all, she was a wonderful wife, mother, and eye surgeon. He began to wonder if maybe he could learn to make his own bologna sandwiches. He'd give it a try.

He munched on his sandwich—a perfect balance of bread, bologna, and mustard, surpassing anything he'd ever tasted in the cafeteria—and analyzed his adventure. He began to feel hopeful. He had been right about the sausage; three years of research had paid off. And if he continued to acquire expertise, maybe someday he'd be like the Experts—always right. Maybe the good guys came out on top in the end by dint of hard work, brains, and skill. He sure hoped so; he had twenty-five more years of this. He picked up a *Pravda Vostoka* article on brass buttons and began reading.

Writing Under PAR

Every organization in the Intelligence Community has some type of Performance Appraisal Report in which employees are evaluated against a standard and each other. Colleagues in the armed forces report the following outtakes from Officer Efficiency Reports:

"Not the sharpest knife in the drawer."

"Got into the gene pool while the lifeguard wasn't watching."

"A room temperature IQ."

"Got a full 6-pack, but lacks the plastic thingy to hold it all together."

"A gross ignoramus—144 times worse than an ordinary ignoramus."

"A photographic memory but with the lens cover glued on."

"A prime candidate for natural de-selection."

"Bright as Alaska in December."

"One-celled organisms outscore him in IQ tests."

"Donated his brain to science before he was done using it."

"Fell out of the family tree."

"Gates are down, the lights are flashing, but the train isn't coming."

"Has two brains: one is lost and the other is out looking for it."

"He's so dense, light bends around him."

"If brains were taxed, he'd get a rebate."

"If he were any more stupid, he'd have to be watered twice a
  week."

"If you give him a penny for his thoughts, you'd get change."

"If you stand close enough to him, you can hear the ocean."

"Some drink from the fountain of knowledge; he only gargled."

"Takes him an hour and a half to watch *60 Minutes*."

"Was left on the Tilt-A-Whirl a bit too long as a baby."

"Wheel is turning, but the hamster is dead."

A second military efficiency report glossary applies to any rank:
How To Interpret Performance Reviews

Some of you might like to know what supervisors are really saying
in all those glowing employee work performance evaluations they
keeps cranking out.

- Average: Not too bright.
- Exceptionally Well Qualified: Has committed no major
  blunders to date.
- Active Socially: Drinks heavily.
- Zealous Attitude: Opinionated.
- Character Above Reproach: Still one step ahead of the law.
- Unlimited Potential: Will stick with us until retirement.
- Quick Thinking: Offers plausible excuses for errors.
- Takes Pride in Work: Conceited.
- Takes Advantage of Every Opportunity To Progress: Buys
  drinks for superiors.
- Indifferent to Instruction: Knows more than superiors.
- Stern Disciplinarian: A real jerk.
- Tactful in Dealing with Superiors: Knows when to keep
  mouth shut.
- Approaches Difficult Problems with Logic: Finds someone
  else to do the job.

- A Keen Analyst: Thoroughly confused.
- Not a Desk Person: Did not attend a university.
- Expresses Self Well: Can string two sentences together.
- Spends Extra Hours on the Job: Miserable home life.
- Conscientious and Careful: Scared.
- Meticulous in Attention to Detail: A nitpicker.
- Demonstrates Qualities of Leadership: Has a loud voice.
- Judgment is Usually Sound: Lucky.
- Maintains Professional Attitude: A snob.
- Keen Sense of Humor: Knows lots of dirty jokes.
- Strong Adherence to Principles: Stubborn.
- Gets Along Extremely Well with Superiors and Subordinates Alike: A coward.
- Slightly Below Average: Stupid.
- Of Great Value to the Organization: Turns in work on time.
- Is Unusually Loyal: Wanted by no-one else.
- Alert to Company Developments: An office gossip.
- Requires Work-Value Attitudinal Readjustment: Lazy and hard-headed.
- Hard Worker: Usually does it the hard way.
- Enjoys Job: Needs more to do.
- Happy: Paid too much.
- Well Organized: Needs more to do.
- Competent: Is still able to get work done if supervisor helps.
- Consults with Supervisor Often: Pain in the arse.
- Will Go Far: Related to management.
- Should Go Far: Please.
- Uses Time Effectively: Clock watcher.
- Very Creative: Finds five reasons to do anything except original work.
- Uses Resources Well: Delegates everything.
- Deserves Promotion: . . . Or anything else—just get him or her away from me!

Some performance appraisals are oral, rather than written down. Among the great observations is this quip, attributed to Bob Gates, describing a prominent colleague as "the kind of man who lights his hair on fire and then beats it out with a hammer."

Other performance appraisals are of a class of people, usually management, rather than of an individual. For example:

When I got into the Agency as a staff officer in 1973, I heard that a defect in the HVAC system of OHB had recently been discovered. It led to a deficiency of oxygen, which was more severe the higher one went in the building. For those of us on lower elevations, this helped explain observed failings of management and estimating. Characteristically, a victim of oxygen deprivation doesn't know it's happening to him.

Historian Crane Brinton, who once served as an OSS analyst, told OSS analytical chief William Langer, "I have no doubt the high point of my career in intelligence came when I was called upon to answer a telephone request for the plural of 'epigloittis.'" I thank Charles Lathrop, compiler of *The Literary Spy,* for reporting that it is either epiglottises or epiglotides.

A senior manager was so upset with the work of one of his female subordinates that he called her a "dumb $%^&." She initiated a grievance against his conduct and he was duly ordered to apologize to her. He apologized to her for calling her a "$%^&" but "dumb" he insisted stood.

From the fall 1991 edition of *Studies in Intelligence* "Writing Below PAR":

In evaluating and ranking individual CIA officers stationed worldwide, Directorate of Operations' promotion panels rely heavily on written Performance Appraisal Reports. Promotion panels, which may have no direct knowledge of the individual in question, use PARs as the primary means to determine performance and potential relative to other officers at that grade. For this reason, each panel looks closely at the accuracy, tenor, and scope of PARs.

PAR writers whose narrative fully and explicitly substantiates the grades assigned to measure performance are commended by evaluation panels. PAR writers whose language is vague, misleading, over-general, or fails to address performance requirements are chastised and shown the error of their ways.

Because of the vast number of PARs reviewed by each panel, infelicitous phrases, malapropos, and mixed metaphors become collectors' items. The examples in this article are drawn from such collections. My occasional observations are in parentheses.

Some Worst Cases

"He managed to conduct a three-hour conversation in a language he had never spoken before." (A neat trick.)

"She is the shining light in the cemetery at night." (The gravedigger, perhaps?)

"The highlight of the period was Subject's tenacious pursuit of an elusive target which cannot further be identified."

"He merits an illegal but descriptive strong 6." (Notify the lawyers!)

"She is the cinderblock which holds this place together."

"Subject must stop trying to act as a male operative and instead capitalize on her advantages as a female in the same role." (Mata Hari lives!)

"On balance, Subject manages to break even."

"She is so good she must be an alien; she couldn't possibly be from planet Earth."

"She was born much too soon and is way ahead of her time; ergo, she is the best we could hope for!"

"This officer cannot be underrated."

"In addition to his strong performance, he manages to deal with the other vagrancies of the job." (A bummer.)

"He is one of the rare breed—a case officer who knows and understands his target." (What does this say about the rest of us?)

"Recently, he has encumbered some difficult cases."

"She is so good it's difficult to determine what she does best."

"I believe he can improve in each of his rated duties, but that this has been a very satisfying beginning which has pleased me, shows demonstrable strengths and fewer areas to develop, and which is a very sound base for the first full year of his tour." (Huh?)

"While she readily seeks guidance herself, she rarely is at a loss for sound suggestions when doing so."

"His face-to-face dealings with ops personnel in another division frequently necessitate his making comments spontaneously, and he does this most competently." (No wires or strings?)

"Not to imply that she is without weaknesses, but I consider it a strength that she will let you know right off the bat when something is outside her ken."

"She is totally reliable, consistently does more than the job calls for, and does it all with a smile on her face." (Let a smile be your umbrella!)

"He could use a tad more patience in his relations with those of his station colleagues who on occasion have different opinions."

"The rotating technical referent position has spun off to another employee." (Whirling dervishes wanted!)

"She frequently displayed good managerial behavior."

"She has an unusually close relationship with the Station's main liaison contact." (Some things are best left unsaid.)

"She never asks her subordinate to do what she is willing to do." (And what is she not willing to do?)

"Subject's new role placed her squarely in the path of incensed analysts and supervisors, any one of whom could have made a powerful enemy." (Were they armed?)

". . . has valiantly battled the impossible and has plied the waves of paper, bureaucracy, and the halls of HQS." (In a boat?)

". . . retries highly sensitive and sometimes volatile records."

"She does not flap."

"When he stubbed his toe, he recovered with grace." (Yes, but can he do the work?)

". . . displays strong interpersonal skills interfacing with colleagues and a savvy understanding of the season." (Plays well with others and knows that it's winter.)

"Subject bore the brunt of their passions with equanimity." (By thinking of England?)

"This is a truly remarkable quality for an officer of his vintage." (Yes, but does he have a full bouquet?)

". . . acted as den mother to four CTs."

". . . a special TDY team tackled and recruited this target." (Drafted from the Redskins?)

"We will miss her bubbly, lilting laugh and fierce loyalty."

"In the best sense of the word, he is a hustler."

"The officer has manifested all the qualities of native intelligence." (How about foreign intelligence?)

"Frequent travel enabled her sharply to detail the synergistic relationship which has developed over the years."

"Subject is a joy to supervise because he requires no supervision." (The ideal employee.)

"He has a definite military bearing; tall, erect, polite, and firm."

"He comes to work and will continue to excel himself."

"She has launched herself on an accelerated trajectory of advancement." (But where will she come down?)

"She has become a multitalented, odd-job man." (A gender-bender.)

"Subject spotted a trend of single females." (Also, a gaggle of geese and a pod of whales!)

"She contributes tremendous hours of uncompensated overtime."

The Last Word(s)

Finally, I offer this compendium of glittering generalities to avoid in writing PARs. Instead of using any of the below, just provide specific and pertinent examples.

"Subject demonstrated . . . sound judgment/accepted additional responsibility/is cost conscious/a team player/is talented/has excellent presence/is unfailingly helpful/can-do and prompt/ steady/well organized/even tempered and tactful/has a keen intellect/is self-disciplined/works smoothly with her peers/ is competent/determined/enthusiastic/cheerful/works with unabated enthusiasm/and indomitable energy/and is one of the few remaining fountains of institutional memory."

From the spring 1994 edition of *Studies in Intelligence,* "More PAR Bloopers":

From time to time the challenge of crafting timely, accurate, and persuasive performance appraisal reports (PARs) strains the skills of the most dedicated and thoughtful manager. The malapropisms, creative misspellings, and mixed metaphors that occasionally result cause both confusion and amusement in centralized Directorate of Operations (DO) evaluation and promotion panels. The following excerpts, selected by 1993 panels, illustrate why English is often cited as a difficult language. Excerpts are grouped according to the panel response they elicited. Our observations are in parentheses:

I Beg Your Pardon?

"X accompanies a majority of meetings the rater attends . . ." (Does X play banjo or piano when accompanying?)

"We cannot miss a beat in this office." (It throws off the aforementioned banjo player.)

"Complimentary to his employee grooming..." (Nothing like making sure that your employees are well coifed, and well complemented.)

"She immediately tightened her belt and effectively performed her duties and those of her subordinates." (A Special Achievement Award for a two-for-one-blooper sentence.)

"X is competent in the completion of memoranda responsive to requests when the results are negative and those which are so vague that it is impossible to conduct a reasonable search." (Translation: "Sorry, we have no idea what you want.")

". . . tomorrow is often a luxury." (Don't tell the IRS. They'll try to tax it.)

". . . during the terrible rotational cycle of 1992 . . ." (Right up there with the blizzard of '88, the flood of '93, and the Mets of '62.)

"The fire in the gut has not always been obvious." (Another satisfied Maalox customer.)

I Don't Think That Word Means What You Think It Means

"His erstwhile contribution and participation is expected to continue." (*Le mot juste.*)

"She possesses good intrapersonal skills." (Talks to herself; gets polite answers.)

"X tackles new assignments willingly." (Okay, X, you rush the quarterback; I'll cover the receivers.)

"One of subject's most attributable assets . . ." (The employee's other assets are not his own.)

"X has demonstrated the capability to perform complex tasks in a qualitative manner." (Written by an economist!)

"Can be called upon on a real-time basis." (Comes when called.)

"X worked concomitantly with OGC..." (The only way to work with OGC.)

"Subject prepared poignant talking points." (Tell your asset her eyes are like limpid pools.)

". . . has an uncanny precognitive response." (Like a preventive reaction strike?)

Is This a Biological Thing?

"Due to his height, this man should probably be directed

along liaison lines or staff work." (Over 6 feet or under 4 feet?)

"He involves himself athletically in Base and local activities." (Physical conditioning is a must.)

"All said and done, Subject is human." (What a relief! We thought he might be an alien.)

"He needs to get the operational chrysalis out of the political cocoon it is in." (A tricky metamorphosis.)

"He is endowed with a certain lethal gentleness." (And she has a certain gentle lethality?)

"He supervises one part-time wife." (If the service had wanted you to have a wife, they would have issued you one.)

"He needs to develop a sense of looking more at the horizon at the front than checking back to see how well he is covered to the rear." (Sounds like this one has executive potential.)

Yes, But What Did They Actually Do?

"X demonstrated an extraordinarily high learning curve." (Did he go ballistic?)

"Subject encouraged and enjoyed a steady stream of visitors to her office, including political officers, DEA officers, military attachés, visiting analysts, and lesser mortals." (Such as? Oh, well, at least she enjoyed them.)

"She has served in a position of furnishing continuous continuity to this base." (Without a break?)

"Subject projects the image of a highly intelligent and professional officer." (Isn't, but projects a great image.)

"Policymakers were indeed literally hanging on her very words, creating constant, extreme pressures." (Hanging is, after all, a capital punishment.)

"One of X's main attributes is that she has the self-confidence to question herself." (Self-debriefing, a great party trick.)

"The highest compliment that can be paid to X . . . was that after her departure . . . the desk was ably handled by a CT." (Okay, what's the second highest?)

"He must keep his eye on the importance of constantly turning over rocks, examining what might be worthwhile underneath and, if there's not much, replacing the rock and moving to the next one. He must learn to be an efficient hunter." (And the rater an efficient writer.)

More Food Metaphors?

"Eager to gain additional knowledge and experience, X consumed every piece of information shared by Y." (Thereby providing food for thought?)

"Managers and employees were starving for her expertise." (Let's get her together with the previous employee and start a food fight.)

"Subject suffers from intellectual malnutrition." (A loser in the last food fight.)

"Can cut through garbage, get to the meat." (Never accept a dinner invitation from this officer.)

Headquarters Versus the Field

"X, who characterizes himself as 'not having a natural warmth for people' and as 'having difficulty communicating,' has a realistic and effective way of conveying his concepts." (In other words, X knows he's a jerk, you know he's a jerk, and he tells you anyway.)

"One recent returnee, a senior officer fresh from several days of Headquarters briefings, commented that Subject's briefing was the only substantive conversation he'd had since returning to Headquarters." (Don't complain, buddy. Imagine what it's like to work with these people every day!)

"The Headquarters-Field relationship is the lifeblood of the DO and Subject's role in the program was the oxygen that provided the fuel and energy." (Calling Dr. Kildare.)

". . . not just another Headquarters Department of Obfuscation . . ." (But THE Headquarters Department of Obfuscation.)

Cliché Count!

". . . no noticeable weaknesses." (Or has kept them hidden so far.)

". . . tenacity of a bulldog." (Doesn't know when it's time to let go.)

". . . fulfills every manager's dream." (Mine is a Ferrari. Can this employee get me one?)

". . . without belaboring a cliché . . ." (Don't worry, it's already been done.)

"Proverbial quick study." (Call Aesop! I can't remember that proverb!)

English is a Difficult Language!

"X is able to identify problems and successfully complete them in its entirety." (Did the writer lose interest in the sentence?)

". . . imminently capable of providing this important function." (Eminently, too.)

"X has done an excellent good job." (Not just fair to middling, mind you.)

". . . exceptionally unique." (Writer is taking PAR-writing lessons from the previous rater.)

". . . a very important necessity." (Glad to see we have another student in that class.)

"It was immediately clear when foreign hands were found in the World Trade Center bombing . . ." (Must have been messy.)

". . . demonstrated unmitigated excellence . . ." (The rest have been mitigating their excellence, and I want it stopped, pronto!)

". . . showed excellent understanding of the English-language." (Glad somebody here does. But what's that hyphen for?)

"X found his self alone." (Without no help?)

"Seldom has such a large accomplishment fit into a single PAR paragraph." (For my next writing trick...)

"I'll-do-as-I'm-told-so-I-can-get-back-overseas trap." (Winner of the adjective of the year award, but don't let this rater near any more hyphens.)

Metaphorically Speaking

". . . provided oral briefs . . ." (I prefer Hanes.)

". . . quintessential diamond in the rough . . ." (Translation: Hard to work with.)

". . . making sure that the release of DO information does not result in an unmanageable mosaic." (Annals of Flowery Prose, Round I.)

"He takes more time than most of his peers to travel from Key Building to Headquarters to community facilities . . ." (Get this guy a horse! A map! Something!)

". . . standing astride the divide between ops and analysis and pitching and catching with both hands . . ." (Quick, call the Orioles!)

"X could squeeze traces out of a rock!" (Concealment devices get more and more clever.)

"X is the spark plug which fires the DCO engine." (On all six cylinders?)

"This PAR is an effort to take the bushel basket away from X's 'light.'" (Words fail us. And failed the rater, too.)

Spell Check!

". . . heroine trafficking . . ." (Low bidder on the spell checker.)

". . . cudo . . ." (I'll hit him with my thesaurus. Kudos is not plural.)

"X has undergone a complete metamorphous . . ." (Back to caterpillars again.)

". . . completed her 3-year trail period . . ." (Presumably somewhere out in the field.)

". . . speedy editorial finallzing . . ." (Glad she wasn't in a hurry to get it done.)

". . . subject's communications abilities . . . and . . . technical fine points . . ." (The gift that keeps on giving.)

". . . more felicitous in style." (Never met a style problem she couldn't lick.)

"Never requires editing for . . . grammer/spelling." (Maybe we can still get our money back on the spell checker.)

"Beyond the cope of her assigned duties . . ." (Such as proofreading?)

". . . expressed herself verbally with equal flare and ease." (Quite a flashy speaker.)

Anchors Aweigh!

"X enthusiastically immersed himself . . ." (Splash! Category S overboard!)

". . . pulling her oar . . ." (A failed attempt to rescue the person above.)

"She has sailed uncharted waters in a nontraditional boat without hitting any rocks." (Woman on board!)

". . . was thrown in at the deep end and performed swimmingly." ("There's a whale in the bathtub," said Tom superficially.)

"X dived in with both feet." (Straight sixes work on PARs here, but not at the Olympics.)

". . . showed persistence and tack." (By fishing in troubled waters.)

What Is Going On Here?

"You are welcome to rotate with us any time." (We go around in bureaucratic circles.)

"X is the third or fourth largest DO station in the world." (Depending upon whether everyone shows up for work on the day we count noses.)

"X had the misfortune of arriving at perhaps the worst period in station's history: its physical destruction." (Of course, there was that one really bad hair day last week.)

"I was impressed, several months ago, with how quickly X understood what I was saying at a briefing." (I mumble a lot.)

"She followed the instructions perfectly, as I knew she would— except for the yelling." (She's still learning to yell.)

". . . she has spread her mantle of efficiency over him as well." (Leaving us all gasping for air.)

"This individual was assassinated before Subject's ops initiatives could be implemented." (If only Subject had met her deadline with that target study!)

"Subject is also very thorough in the execution." (Just tell that to the officer above!)

". . . extensive network of contacts within the outside of the Directorate . . ." (Is this person going up the down staircase?)

". . . with . . . development . . . of a unilateral surveillance team running close behind." (The team is training for the Olympics.)

"Laziness and greed began to pose handling problems." (Another great vaudeville team.)

"She takes the time to proofread her work and the results show." (Whiteout all over the page.)

"A CT . . . who sincerely thought a sanitized memo has to be first boiled to remove fingerprints." (We do that only to get the whiteout off.)

Math Check!

"X ran 264 traces, three times more than the 145 she ran last year." (Okay, if I have three apples and give you one . . .)

"The newly formed 9-person X branch . . . tripled in size . . . at one point numbered 23 people." (Must be new math.)

". . . On 38 occasions, X displayed a high degree of tact and diplomacy." (As for the other 98,239 occasions . . .)

"Although X is only 11 days past the 120 day rule for writing a PAR, it is my pleasure to report that her performance has continued in the same manner as reported in her previous PAR." (Sets a standard by which all non-sequiturs will be evaluated.)

". . . numberous experts in the cue . . ." (Sounds like a job for a mathematician.)

Call the IG

". . . exercising an increasingly firm grip on her IS-3 reports secretary." (You're choking me!)

". . . (our office) recognized his talents and capabilities by awarding him several EPAs. While these are awarded on a fairly regular basis throughout the DO . . ." (Hey, it keeps him happy . . .)

"Ms. Subject's . . ." (Well, it may be politically correct.)

"Mr. Subject." (Apparently the spouse/brother of Ms. Subject.)

Please, Don't Say It Again!

"Which brings me to a point that I simply cannot overemphasize." (But watch me. These are not idle words.)

"As I have stated over and over, but feel it is worth repeating . . ." (Would you mind saying that again?)

". . . leaving me with little to add." (The reviewer then went on for 1½ pages.)

"She exhibits no weaknesses which require improvement." (They're strong weaknesses in their own right.)

Pointing Out the Obvious

". . . her job changed and evolved during her tour." (Evolution without change. What a concept!)

"For the record, in this Rater's thirty-one years with the Agency as a Category B officer, he has written only three overall seven PARs." (This was not one of them, but thanks for setting the record straight.)

"Tedious it is, but it is the only way." (The Tao of Tedium.)

"She has the potential to be rated higher, depending upon her future performance." (How do *you* spell "tautology"?)

". . . on arrival here, X's duties were new to him." A surprise party? You shouldn't have!)

Aerial Surveillance and Other Air Stories

Intelligence isn't just case officers recruiting spies and analysts writing papers for policy makers. Those who conduct aerial surveillance, at various altitudes, have their own style of humor, samples of which appear below.

The motto of the A-12 (you know them as SR-71 Blackbird surveillance planes) alumni association: In God We Trust. All others we monitor.

—Rules for Test Pilots for Surveillance planes:

1. Try to stay in the middle of the air.
2. Do not go near the edges of it.
3. The edges of the air can be recognized by the appearance of ground, buildings, sea, trees, and interstellar space. It is much more difficult to fly there.

—From an OXCART A-12 pilot who overflew hostile territory a year before the multi-crew SR-71: "Though I fly through the Valley of Death, I shall fear no Evil for I am at 90,000 feet and climbing."

—In a famous SR-71 story, Los Angeles Center reported receiving a request for clearance to 60,000 feet. The incredulous controller, with some disdain in his voice, asked, "How do you plan to get up to 60,000 feet?" The pilot responded, "We don't plan to go up to it, we plan to go down to it." He was cleared.

Standard Operating Procedures for Flight Operations:

Takeoffs are optional. Landings are mandatory.

If God meant man to fly, He'd have given him more money.

If you push the stick forward, the houses get bigger; if you pull the stick back, they get smaller. (Unless you keep pulling the stick back; then they get bigger again.)

Flying is not dangerous; crashing is dangerous.

It's better to be down here wishing you were up there, than up there wishing you were down here.

The propeller is just a big fan in the front of the plane to keep the pilot cool. Want proof? Make it stop; then watch the pilot break out into a sweat.

Speed is life; altitude is life insurance. No one has ever collided with the sky.

It's best to keep the pointed end going forward as much as possible.

The only time you have too much fuel is when you're on fire.

Flying is the second greatest thrill known to man. . . . Landing is the first!

A "good" landing is one from which you can walk away. A "great" landing is one after which you can use the airplane another time.

The probability of survival is equal to the angle of arrival.

Always remember: you fly an airplane with your head, not your hands.

Never let an airplane take you somewhere your brain didn't get to five minutes earlier.

You know you've landed with the wheels up when it takes full power to taxi.

Those who hoot with the owls by night should not fly with the eagles by day.

A helicopter is a collection of rotating parts going round and round and reciprocating parts going up and down—all of them trying to become random in motion.

Helicopters can't really fly—they're just so ugly that the earth immediately repels them.

"Young man, was that a landing or were we shot down?"

Learn from the mistakes of others. You won't live long enough to make all of them yourself.

Trust your captain, but keep your seat belt securely fastened.

Any pilot who relies on a terminal forecast can be sold the Brooklyn Bridge. If he relies on winds-aloft reports he can be sold Niagara Falls.

Good judgment comes from experience and experience comes from bad judgment.

Aviation is not so much a profession as it is a disease.

There are three simple rules for making a smooth landing: Unfortunately, no one knows what they are.

The only thing worse than a captain who never flew as copilot is a copilot who once was a captain.

Be nice to your first officer; he may be your captain at your next airline.

Any attempt to stretch fuel is guaranteed to increase headwind.

A thunderstorm is never as bad on the inside as it appears on the outside. It's worse.

"Son, I was flying airplanes for a living when you were still in liquid form."

It's easy to make a small fortune in aviation. You start with a large fortune.

A male pilot is a confused soul who talks about women when he's flying, and about flying when he's with a woman.

A fool and his money are soon flying more airplane than he can handle.

Remember, you're always a student in an airplane.

Keep looking around; there's always something you've missed.

Try to keep the number of your landings equal to the number of your takeoffs.

You cannot propel yourself forward by patting yourself on the back.

There are old pilots, and there are bold pilots, but there are no old, bold pilots!

Things which do you no good in aviation:
- Altitude above you.
- Runway behind you.
- Fuel in the truck.
- Half a second ago.
- Approach plates in the car.
- The airspeed you don't have.
- The pee bottle locked in the baggage compartment/another airplane/hangar.
- Tow bar attached as you takeoff.
- Unattached gas caps.
- Cowl plugs attached as you roll.

Flying is the perfect vocation for a man who wants to feel like a boy, but not for one who still is.

Asking what a pilot thinks about the FAA is like asking a fireplug what it thinks about dogs.

Being an airline pilot would be great if you didn't have to go on all those trips.

Gravity never loses! The best you can hope for is a draw.

Of course, aerial surveillance was not the only use of air capabilities in intelligence work. The pilots and staff of Air America conducted thousands of flights in support of our operations in the Southeast Asian war. Check out their Web site, www.air-america. org, for details after reading these reminiscences by former station manager Charlie Griffith:

Some Telephone Poles at Danang Airport

In the mid-sixties when I was once on TDY to Danang as acting SZ while Gil Stafford was on Home Leave, there came a need to move some unusually long telephone poles by air from a U.S. Naval facility on the other side of the bay away from the airport area and seaport. These were much too long to be moved by truck.

So it came to be that using a helicopter was the best way to do the moving. I forget the crew members' names and what type of 'chopper we used, but it was very tricky business as anyone with more knowledge than I have can verify. There was also a need for someone extra to go along to the other side and connect the chain attached to the pole to the hovering a/c's special hook underneath.

I volunteered to do that. With the 'chopper hovering gently inches over my hunched shoulders I managed to do the deed then run out from under and give a "thumbs-up." Everything worked well, and they airlifted three of those poles over to the antenna-farm site near the airport. When I got back to our "office" in a building on the airfield, I had a terse, adrenaline-stimulated message sent to my boss, Merrill Hulse, in Saigon, and said ". . . Pleased to announce three successful erections today, hopefully another one tomorrow." Merrill's reply was, ". . . At your age you should be thankful."

Wild Orchid Search, Central Laos

Yes, this actually happened, and I leave it to your collective hindsight imagination to think of its potential for maximum trouble. While at Savannakhet sometime during 1967-68, someone (perhaps me) came up with the idea while sitting around the hostel one afternoon of going out to search in the boonies for wild orchids which could be pulled by their roots from the side of a tree. As air-plants, they'd grow onto any place where their seeds blew which also afforded them shelter. I volunteered to drive our station jeep. So I think about three of the Volpar Aerial Survey Project Pilots and myself said, "Sure, why not? Beats sitting here!" We set out along dusty, potholed roads a pretty good distance from the outskirts of Savannakhet, and for quite some time. After a while we found some orchids and pried them away from the tree with long poles and got them undamaged and with good blooms into the jeep, and later back to the hostel. I remember putting mine in the small shower stall I had at my quarters a three-minute walk away. Others sitting in the hostel, who hadn't seen us leave, said "You've been *where?* Doing *what?*"

Overhead surveillance sometimes doesn't require an aircraft. The whole Hardy Boys-type sons of a Deputy Chief of Station were playing on the roof of an eight-story building. At one point, they came running back to their parents' apartment to announce to their mother that they had witnessed a naked couple on a rooftop several buildings away, and that "they were doing it!" When their mom asked if they had been spotted, they proclaimed, "Not until we started yelling at them!"

In November 1956, I was assigned to Detachment 10-10, the U-2 project at Incirlik Air Base in Adana, Turkey. Despite having only recently arrived, I was selected, having drawn the appropriately sized straw, to escort to Washington the classified take from a recent overflight. The take typically consisted of two rather big boxes and a few smaller packages. I was to proceed from Adana to our sister detachment in Giebelstadt, Germany, from whence I would be taken by vehicle to Rhein Main Air Base to connect with a special flight to Dover Delaware Air Base, then to be trucked to Washington to deliver materials to the Steuart Building. I would be armed with a snub-nosed .38 pistol in a shoulder holster, which would remain concealed except in an emergency, and some Mickey Mouse orders identifying me as a USAF civilian courier, GS-12. (As a relatively new GS-7, I found this morale-enhancing.)

The first leg in our detachment aircraft was uneventful. It would prove to be the only leg that was. Arriving early evening at Giebelstadt, I joined some friends for dinner at the club. At some point, Col. Fred McCoy, Detachment Commander, came to our table to introduce himself. He said he would be flying to Rhein Main the following morning, a forty-five-minute flight as opposed to a five-hour drive, and I was welcome to join him. Always on the alert for a good deal, I promptly recognized one and accepted.

Very early the next day, I was out on the air strip to supervise the loading of my cargo onto the aircraft, an L-20 with USAF markings. An L-20 is a single engine prop plane, a two-seater with a high wing that looks like a boxy Piper Cub. Soon we were airborne. I was in the right seat with a top coat hiding my weapon, and Col. McCoy was in the pilot's seat, in full uniform and displaying rows of ribbons topped by Command Pilot wings.

About an hour into the forty-five-minute flight, I asked, "Are we there yet?" Col. McCoy responded that he was having trouble finding Rhein Main, that it was apparently enveloped by a lot of ground fog and neither our radio nor homing device were operating. So we bored holes in the sky for a little while, sometimes turning left and sometimes right. Suddenly, something roared over the top of our right wing and disappeared in the sky before us, leaving a massive turbulence in its wake. This was repeated three or four times. Col. McCoy speculated that they were USAF F-102s, trying to lead us into Rhein Main, which did not seem feasible, since we were so slow and they were so fast. After this little caper came to an end, Col. McCoy announced that he was returning to Giebelstadt.

An hour later, with some trepidation, I asked the same question as before. The good Colonel advised that he was unable to find Giebelstadt, that we were getting low on gas, and I should keep my eyes open for an airstrip—any airstrip. Within minutes I spotted a small strip and we headed for it. As we taxied along, we saw a small Quonset hut with stars and bars on it and a little Army plane much like ours sitting next to it. We pulled in and while the Colonel was looking for a phone, I rousted a GI who was napping in the hut and asked him if he had any gas. He said he could probably scrounge up twenty or thirty gallons in five gallon cans. So we got out a funnel and took all the gas he had. Meanwhile, Col. McCoy advised that we were just a few miles south of Giebelstadt and all we had to do was follow the main highway right to the front gate.

After 20 minutes in the air, I could see no highway, and, well, I won't bore you with the dialogue. In any event, Giebelstadt was nowhere in sight and the Colonel advised me that we now had a serious fuel problem. He asked if I wanted to jump! Noting that we didn't seem to have much altitude, I asked what his plans were. He said he was going to "ride it on in." I elected to do likewise. He then asked if I could tell which way the wind was blowing. At that point, we were heading toward what appeared to be a small village surrounded by open pasture. I could see some laundry hanging in yards, and I would report the wind blowing one way, then another. Absorbed in my meteorological duties, I suddenly realized that things had become very quiet. (Dead engines will cause that phenomenon.) So we headed for a pasture, made ground contact with a huge thud, roared along right through a big pile of hay, and finally came to a halt only feet from a high stone wall. (I learned later that the village cemetery was on the other side of the wall. I also noted later some high tension wires that we had apparently gone under when we landed.) After I congratulated Col. McCoy (we never did get on a first-name basis) on the landing, he decided he would go off on another phone-finding mission in the village. I, of course, had to stay with my classified cargo.

As he was leaving, the villagers were arriving. A huge crowd encircled the aircraft. (If a foreign plane landed in your backyard, wouldn't you come out to see what was going on?) My major concern was the cargo, but I could also see that some of them were intent on getting a souvenir and I was trying to prevent them from hacksawing a piece from the propeller. It was a gray, misty, cold day and my feet in my little Thom McCanns were freezing as I circled around the frozen tundra. Then some of them got the bright idea to board the aircraft. I managed to beat them to it and then decided that my best bet was to stay inside the plane and hope that would deter the crowd. I had already concluded that to display my weapon would only make matters worse. And so I sat, wondering where the Colonel was and eyeballing the assemblage, which seemed to have concluded that I was some sort of lunatic as they pointed at me, shaking their heads and making clucking sounds.

After a considerable period of time, the Colonel reappeared. He had found a phone, contacted Giebelstadt and advised that they would arrive to pick us up. (It turned out that we were in a town called Friesing, which was not far from where we wanted to be.) He had apparently found a cozy little gasthaus, had a few pops, and bonded with the patrons, who now formed an admiring entourage as they followed behind him.

Eventually, a security team led by Jack Harris arrived in a Volkswagen bus. First priority, however, was to rescue Harris. He had attempted to leap over a rather fast-running stream not far from the lane, landed right in the middle of it, and washed up a little bit down stream. The stream was about fifteen or twenty feet wide, so it would have been a feat of Olympic proportions had he made it. At any rate, the boys loaded my cargo and off we went to Giebelstadt. I had flown all day and gone nowhere. I later learned at Happy Hour that we had been tracked on radar the entire time and our erratic movements had everybody worried, because we were very close to the East zone. The thought even occurred that we had turned off all our electronics and were trying to defect with our precious cargo. The F-102s had been ordered to shoot us down if it appeared that we were attempting to cross into the East! The next day I went by road to Rhein Main and boarded a special flight to Dover. The festivities weren't over.

The special flight was a C-54, a four-engine prop plane. It was carrying a bunch of coffins, presumably occupied, and me and my cargo. At some point late in the flight, the crew chief awakened me from a nap and advised that we had lost the left outboard engine. I was exhausted and not fully comprehending and mumbled something about waking me again if we lost any more. I was awakened again when the crew chief advised that the right outboard engine had shut down. I was now paying attention. He suggested that I get off the floor and buckle myself into one of the bucket seats, which I did, without a word. I remained there until we landed, departing the aircraft to find it surrounded by emergency vehicles of every shape and size. As my cargo was being loaded on the Steuart vehicle, I noted the crew chief eyeing me suspiciously, probably thinking that if I wasn't simply stupid, as a civilian I had behaved reasonably well to avoid panic in a fairly difficult situation. What he didn't know was where I had been in the last few days and that I was neither stupid nor courageous, just numb.

During jump training in 1976, we shook up the rookies on the ground when we dropped a dummy out of the airplane. He had a long red scarf streaming behind him, but no parachute. When he crashed to earth, a medic ran to his side and beat on his chest to amplify the effect.

O'Toole's: A Reminiscence of a KUBARK Institution

by Anonymous

This is a story of a simpler and a happier time, a time before Global Warming, a time before Overseas Contingency Operations and Man-Caused Disasters, a time before Fusion, a time before Smugness. The events in this story took place in the last century, a time that is rapidly fading into the mists of apathy and neglect. This is an effort to preserve at least one small part of that time.

Although a simpler and a happier time, there nevertheless occurred at that time a titanic, protracted, drawn-out and really long struggle: a struggle in which, as it was a simpler and happier time, the force lines were clearly drawn and delineated. This was a struggle between Good and Evil, Right and Wrong, Beneficence and Malevolence, between Us and Them. This struggle was known as the Cold War and those who waged it on Our Side, as Cold Warriors. They were a proud, noble, fierce, dedicated and a really good bunch of people and this is part of their story.

This small group of brave, stalwart, intrepid, worthy, dedicated and really good people was known as KUBARK. The forces of the other side, the side of Evil, Wrong, Malevolence and Them, took the form of a force of perfidious, invidious, nasty, brutish, thuggish and really bad people; they were known as the Dirty Commie Bastards (DCB). This is the story of one small part of the struggle between KUBARK and the DCB.

In that simpler and happier time, KUBARK was located in a Very Large Pile of Gray Granite in McLean, Virginia, known, for some reason to everyone who did not work there, as 'Langley.' Difficult as it may be to believe today, KUBARK was a secret organization. This meant that not a lot of people knew about it, what it did or, for the most part, who did it. Even its name was known to only a very few, to the anointed. What was not known even then and is only now being told for the first time, is the story of the existence of a secret group within the secret organization, a small coterie of elite, dedicated, hard-working, stalwart, intrepid and really good people who labored throughout the Cold War to defeat the DCB and the fact that this was ultimately accomplished stands as testimony to the success of their efforts. This is their story.

KUBARK itself provided the cover [see note] for this secret group within a secret organization, the name of which even now, cannot be told. It will be known here simply as The Secret Group (TSG). TSG members traveled daily from the Very Large Pile of Gray Granite to a secret location within a secret location within even yet another secret location. It was there that TSG met and it was there that it crafted the strategies and the tactics that were carried out internationally, globally, beyond our borders and really all of the world to face, counter and defeat the DCB, and the fact that the Cold War was ultimately won by Our Side stands as testimony to the success of their efforts. This is the story of that location.

[*Note:* "Cover" was a device, now largely considered quaint and out-moded, used in those simpler and happier times to conceal people or activities—the existence of which was better not known to one's adversaries. Cover consisted of contriving a story or legend for a secret activity to provide an innocuous and plausible explanation for it to the uninitiated. Thus would the secret activity be "covered." In addition to providing the explanation, the best cover story would actually divert or distract the attention of the unwitting observer away from the secret activity onto something interesting to him but totally innocuous. The concept of cover is an historical relic and exists now only in fictionalized accounts of the era. Excellent and finely preserved examples of cover can be found in the Spy Museum.]

In those simple, happier times, there stood in downtown McLean, Virginia, a modest cinder block, brick-fronted one-story building. A sign outside identified it as the McLean Restaurant. Earlier, it had been known as Bill's Seafood Restaurant and portions of that sign too were still visible. To the TSG, however, the site was known—and only now can it be told—as O'Toole's. This, it is seen, was a cover within a cover within a cover. On the prior page is a contemporaneous, now historical photograph of O'Toole's, made available for the first time by a surviving and charter member of TSG. This is the story of O'Toole's.

TSG had introduced an innovative device into the concept of cover in that O'Toole's was actually run as a functioning restaurant. Although the device was used here successfully throughout the Cold War, there is no evidence that it ever caught on or was used anywhere else, ever again. O'Toole's was Jon Francis (Jack) O'Toole (JOT) who, in addition to providing cover for the venue—and this is now being told only for the first time—was actually the Chief of TSG (C/TSG). This is his story, too.

As one device to support the cover of O'Toole's, the TSG devised and carried out a black propaganda operation, in which a spurious newspaper restaurant review of O'Toole's was prepared and disseminated. The success of this operation was phenomenal, and hundreds if not thousands of copies of the review were reproduced by Thermofax ("burn a copy") in the Very Large Pile of Gray Granite and disseminated informally to KUBARK installations all over the world. It is only now being acknowledged that this was a TSG operation and a copy of that review, also from the archives of a TSG charter member, appears on the next page.

TSG personnel left the Very Large Pile of Gray Granite daily, individually or in small groups, and traveled to O'Toole's where they met and carried out their deliberations. Cover for their meetings was lunch, and their conference table was cleverly disguised as a semi-circular faux mahogany beer bar, removed from the booths and main body of the restaurant. Every day, for the duration of the Cold War, innocent, unwitting civilians enjoyed their burgers, fries and beers, unaware that, mere feet away, their safety, their well-being, indeed their very survival were being protected and defended by the stalwart, intrepid, dedicated, forthright, and swell members of TSG, and that the perfidious, invidious, nasty and really bad efforts of the DCB were daily being met and countered. This is that story.

The TSG met every day and daily plotted the course of the Cold War and their ever increasing and increasingly successful attacks on the DCB. Members of the TSG traveled frequently and worldwide, on the business of KUBARK, but also carrying out TSG missions within their KUBARK missions. TSG communications were by human courier only, thus no written record exists either of its existence or its successes. Both, of course, are amply demonstrated by the eventual and ultimate demise of the DCB and this must stand as a lasting tribute to their efforts. This is part of that story.

The TSG labored for years, its members changing and rotating as they themselves went out on their KUBARK assignments. New members were from time to time added to the rolls, but only after a most serious vetting and assessment procedure. Membership standards for TSG were extremely high and jealously maintained and only the very finest of KUBARK's people qualified.

Years passed, the Cold War continued as TSG work began to bear fruit. Gradually, inexorably, almost imperceptibly, so slow you almost couldn't really notice, the DCB began to weaken, first in one part of the world, then in another, then in several, until that happy day when the Wall came down and people of right thinking, good upbringing, firm character and resolute spirit rejoiced. The others, those of mean spirit, dark souls, and bad complexions, the really bad people, lamented. The job of the TSG, at least for that time, was finished and, although the members continued to assemble from time to time, their ranks inevitably dwindled until the day that O'Toole's ceased to exist; that day, in these annals of the TSG, marks the end of the Cold War.

TSG personnel dispersed (some diverged), some to other duties, some into deserved and delayed retirements, and others we know not where. They received neither parades nor decorations and would have declined them had they been offered. They do, all of them, bask in the satisfaction of knowing that when, while bouncing them on their knees, their little grandsons ask, "What did you do in the great Cold War?" they do not have to reply, "Well, I did name traces in the Very Large Pile of Gray Granite."

Some members of TSG, some of them alas now deceased, can be identified here by first names and for the first time: Burr, Boo, Sy, Lou, Ray, Jack, t'Other Jack, Hav, Paul, Don, Zeke, Rich. Other members either cannot yet be acknowledged or have faded into the mists of memory. They were all a dedicated, stalwart, upstanding, tenacious, hard-working, intrepid and a really good group and this has been their story.

Postscript

With the end of the Cold War, KUBARK too faded from the scene and now no longer exists. The Very Large Pile of Gray Granite has become a Center for the Study of the Legal and Global Implications of Nuance and Empathy. Earnest, bright, eager, young and really naïve attorneys are engaged in a new monumental struggle: the struggle to convince the world that the events of all its earlier history were mere anomalies and that our country is one of empathy, compassion, moderation, understanding and really good stuff. But that is another column for another day.

Copy of spurious newspaper restaurant review, also from the archives of a TSG charter member:

Supping

by Sidney Schiesskopf

[*Note:* Scheisskopf, a drop-out from the Dino G. Angostini School of Ethnic Cooking and Reformed Baptist Church, is the author of several letters to the editor. He is also a frequent eater.]

O'Toole's McLean Inn:

A Nice Place to Visit

Middle American/Gaelic cuisine. Lunch main courses 15 cents to $2.95; open for dinner, but no food served.

6671 Old Dominion Dr., McLean, Virginia 356-XXXX. Closed Sunday. Lunch at various times almost every day Monday through Saturday. The restaurant is open for dinner but the kitchen is not. No credit cards or reservations; come early and bring cash.

Food: (-:

Style: (two whisks)

Value: $$

O'Toole's McLean Inn, formerly—and to some extent still—known as Bill's Seafood Restaurant—quintessentially exemplifies the kind of atmosphere—and atmospherics—which used to pervade New York's Hell's Kitchen. It recalls the byegone era of saloon dining which was typified by a ringing telephone and a nasal voice answering, "Duffy's Tavern. Archie the manager speaking, Duffy ain't here." If Archie and Duffy were still with us, they would be found at O'Toole's.

The Inn, situated in the heart of beautiful downtown McLean, abuts a hardware store and sits astride a dubious printing establishment. In season, Christmas trees are available in the parking lot, as is fresh produce—and some not so fresh—in other seasons. It is a vista for all year, including winter, when the limbs of trees are etched against the sky and asphalt. The Inn's windows have been arranged to take full advantage of the view of the parking lot and Old Dominion Drive itself, along which the leisurely diner can watch the ever-changing procession of commuter vehicles, delivery vans, police cars and garbage trucks. Indeed, its environs provide much of the atmosphere of the Inn itself.

Inside, the Inn's earthy ambiance is a pleasing—and certainly interesting—combination of well-aged formica and linoleum, a mélange of tubular aluminum and some folding chairs, and antique table cloths. The dominant thrust of the décor is decidedly Irish and the generous use of various shades and tones of green is even occasionally reflected in both the food and the patrons. The Inn can comfortably sit fifty people, including twelve stalls at the unpolished bar, although a recent and memorable St. Patrick's Day saw the capacity expand to 658 enthusiastic merrymakers, two Poles and a Lithuanian. A handsome cigarette machine dominates the approach to the tastefully appointed men's and women's toilets which, incidentally, can be used interchangeably.

We have previously noted in these pages that a truly fine eatery is a reflection of its proprietor, and this is certainly true in this case. John Francis ("Jack") O'Toole, known to his regular customers simply as "Mr. O'Toole, Sir" is always on the premises—almost always—a sure sign (usually) of a well-run establishment. The genial host is suave, dignified and urbane, whether presiding over the dispensing of beer at the bar or supervising the activities of the dedicated and talented kitchen staff. Mr. O'Toole, Sir, gained his formidable knowledge of haute cuisine on the streets and in the blind pigs of old New York and it is easy to see that the talents and skills thereby acquired have not at all been affected by their removal to northern Virginia.

At a recent lunch on a rainy Monday, my companion and I were greeted by Mr. O'Toole, Sir, uttering something about all the chicken being in the cafeteria. We didn't know what it meant and assume it to have been some sort of Gaelic blessing. I chose the specialty of the day—as it is every day—chile con carne (beans with meat). It was tastefully served in a surplus United States Coast Guard soup bowl and was pleasingly topped with a cup and a half of freshly chopped onions (the staff prides itself on the fact that all onions are either chopped or sliced on the premises, more often than not on the same day they are served) and came complete with saltines and a spoon. With the addition of several healthy doses of Tabasco sauce (a la carte) it was practically edible, although it did have a tendency later to produce some truly remarkable phenomena in the gastro-intestinal system.

My companion had another specialty, bean soup, whimsically referred to by the proprietor as "soop dejour." It was served in the same manner—but twenty minutes later—and was reported to have produced many of the same internal reactions. With lunch we shared a bowl of French Fried potatoes, "Irish caviar," which are served complete with skins and blemishes, thereby preserving the inherent flavor of both the tubers themselves and the good earth in which they were grown. The host assured us that the grease in the deep fryer is changed several times a year and I find that easy to believe. Our lunch was accompanied by a pitcher of draft beer (the Inn serves only Schlitz beer on draft!) which was served foaming in a chilled pitcher. Chilled but not washed.

A word about the beer mugs. Mr. O'Toole, Sir, is the fortunate owner of a priceless set of early American beer mugs designed by the early American beer mug designer, Reuben Chipp (who also gave his name to the sandwich) and indeed each mug is seen to carry the designer's unmistakable and highly individualistic signature.

On another occasion, my guest had a hamburger "all the way." This American classic is served with relish, lettuce, tomato and onion in an untoasted bun, the whole topped with a generous dollop of Miracle Whip Salad Dressing. It presents such an imposing challenge that the waiter found it necessary to keep his thumb firmly on top to prevent its falling apart while being served. It is served with two paper napkins. A variation of the hamburger, the cheeseburger, in which a single slice of Kraft Velveeta is artfully draped over the meat pattie an instant before its removal from the grill, is also available, at 15 cents extra.

On this occasion I chose the shrimp in a basket. The crustaceans, although once frozen, had been thoroughly thawed for several days before being plunged into the boiling grease. The colorful plastic basket in which they were presented added a note of gaiety to the brownness of the shrimp. A generous serving and not over-priced at $2.95, although it was necessary to request a knife and fork which were thoughtfully wiped on an almost fresh paper napkin before being slid down the bar.

In addition to menu items, special requests are also handled. A recent patron, for example, requested a bacon, lettuce and tomato sandwich without toast. His order was honored, almost without comment.

For those with limited appetites or delicate stomachs, Planters peanuts are a bargain at 15 cents per attractive cellophane bag.

Service is sporadic, but generally good-natured.

Draft and bottle beer; the wine list includes Royal Crown Cola, Fresca, and Diet Pepsi. A limited range of Dutch Master cigars is from time to time available for the discerning smoker.

Miscellany

Stuff that I couldn't categorize but was too good to pass up

Actual Headline (Dave Barry and I swear I am not making this up): "Attorney to seek security clearance for 9/11 defendant at Guantanamo" Andrew O. Selsky, Associated Press, SignOnSanDiego. com June 17, 2008.

Best news media sourcing: In an MSNBC.com article on the continuing investigation of Former Executive Director Kyle "Dusty" Foggo and his colleague, Brent Wilkes, the writer referred to "a source close to the Wilkes poker circle."

Aphorism from KGB chief Sudoplatov: "If your operation is going according to your plan, it probably means that the opposition is in control." Essence: If Murphy (of Murphy's Law), the Lord of Misadventure, is not screwing you up, it means he's working for your opponent to wreck you big time in the end game.

Having just moved into his new office, a self-important new branch chief was sitting at his desk when he heard a knock on the door. Conscious of his new position, the branch chief quickly picked up the phone, told the individual to enter, then said into the phone, "Yes, DCI, I'll be seeing him this afternoon and I'll pass along your message. In the meantime, thank you for your good wishes, sir." Feeling as though he had sufficiently impressed the young man, he asked, "What do you want?"

"Nothing important, sir," the young man replied, "I'm just here to hook up your telephone."

Our brand new facility was touted as the most "green" friendly installation ever created in the USG. It had carpets made from recycled material, a rooftop garden that was the source of the cafeteria's salads, a waterfall of recycled water, even flushless urinals in the men's rooms (the less said about the latter, the better). But the designers of the building did not notice the demographic composition of its inhabitants. Its denizens belonged to the Office of Human Resources, which is overwhelmingly female. But the designers created women's and men's restrooms with the same number of stalls. This of course led to seemingly interminable queues to the women's rooms—not unlike what one experiences in typical sporting events in the US. But the design flaw continued down to the Supply Room. The char force dutifully put the same number of rolls of toilet paper in each stall. Alas, we were able to set our watches to the 2 p.m. screams emanating from the women's room "We're out of G-D toilet paper again!" Women were forced to bring their own—a charming addition to cubicle décor—or surreptitiously sneak into the men's room to liberate their TP. Luckily, we're trained in sneaking around . . .

In August 2001, OHB had a minor fire in which the burn chutes acted as a chimney, at times ushering the fire into the adjoining men's rooms. The female photographer for the Agency's newsletter, *What's News at CIA*, seeing the opportunity for a great photo of the charred rooms, ran into the seventh floor men's room armed with camera, to the great surprise of denizens of the seventh floor, who had ignored the yellow police tape strung across the doorway.

A nineteen-year-old from West Virginia was the secretary for nineteen DI analysts, including one who was hosting two guests from London. The analyst walked out of the office leaving the two Brits unattended to go pick up a book from the Library. A few minutes later he calls the secretary and asks her to go ask the portly gentleman what his name is. The secretary has an Uncle Porty and so she assumes the gentleman's name must be Mr. _____ Portly. So she goes into the room and asks the two Brits, "Which one of you is Mr. Portly?" Both gentlemen look at each other (the one guy rather chubby) smile and respond, "Why, neither one of us is named Mr. Portly." The secretary goes back to the phone and says, "I'm sorry, neither one of their names is Portly." The sound on the other end of the phone is one of hysteria and the analyst says, "Oh my God, you didn't ask if the *name* was portly, did you?" At that moment there was an epiphany in the secretary . . . and she realizes "portly" was not the name.

One day Secretary One was typing at her computer with a badge hanging from her back and a temporary badge clipped to her front. Secretary Two asks, "Why do you have a badge on your back?" to which Secretary One jumps up and yells, "Oh no, I don't have a badge on my back, do I? I got a temporary badge because I couldn't find my own badge."

Shortly after I was brought into the Agency as a staff officer in April 1973 by Schlesinger to be one of his special assistants, I was tasked to redraft an NIE on Soviet strategic doctrine and policy. We'd only signed the first SALT agreements and the Soviets pickled off test firings of three new MIRVed ICBMs. So we launched into a very serious inquiry about what thinking really animated their behavior, leading to the B-Team episodes and a lot more. When the IC team gathered in the oxygen-deprived conference room on the seventh floor of OHB, one of the team suggested that we call this NIE "Deep Threat." This was a take-off on the porno film "Deep Throat" making headlines at the time. Instead, we called it "What are they up to." It has been largely declassified. The NIE team member referred to above, then an ONE staffer, related that, when he underwent his EOD poly, he was asked whether he'd ever spent much time in communist controlled territory. He admitted that he (like I) had gone to Harvard and lived in Cambridge, MA for some years. The polygrapher was not amused. A sense of humor disqualifies people for that work.

There's an old saying that there is no such thing as a stupid question. Maybe not, but there can definitely be a stupid time to ask it.

In the 1970s, DDI Ed Proctor was giving an address in the Headquarters Auditorium. He talked at some length about the implications of the United States getting basing rights on Diego Garcia, a strategically located island in the Indian Ocean. At the end of his speech, the DDI had a question-and-answer session. A journeyman-level analyst who should have known better raised his hand, stood up, and asked, "Sir, who is Diego Garcia?" The DDI stood motionless, and a stunned silence fell over the Auditorium. Finally, the DDI said, "Son, I will assume that you asked that question in all sincerity." And then he moved on to the next question.

"Once in a while, just often enough to give intelligence officers a false sense of confidence, a secret operation goes almost according to plan."

—Former CIA Operations Officer William Hood

"The United States must retain the capability to do something in between sending in the Marines and sending in former President Carter."

—Former DCI R. James Woolsey

Former senior DO officer Burton Lee Gerber observed, "FBI agents are trained to think like bank guards. CIA officers are trained to think like bank robbers."

Naval officers tell their rookies, "There are three kinds of intelligence: human, animal, and naval."

W.J. Holmes in *Double-Edged Secrets*, his memoir on World War II, recalls that intelligence officers sometimes were more than ignored: "In some battleships . . . the most important duty assigned to new combat intelligence officers was keeping track of ship's laundry when the ship was in port."

Two ladies went to an out building for a visit and the windows were so clean that Lady One walked straight into the window and her body flew up in the air in slow motion and she fell backwards on the ground. Lady Two asked, "What were you thinking?"

You Might Be a Taliban, If . . .
1. You refine heroin for a living, but you have a moral objection to beer.

2. You own a $3,000 machine gun and $5,000 rocket launcher, but you can't afford shoes.

3. You have more wives than teeth.

4. You wipe your butt with your bare left hand, but consider bacon "unclean."

5. You think vests come in two styles: bullet-proof and suicide.

6. You can't think of anyone you *haven't* declared Jihad against.

7. You consider television dangerous but routinely carry explosives in your clothing.

8. You were amazed to discover that cell phones have uses other than setting off roadside bombs.

9. You've often uttered the phrase, "I love what you've done with your cave."

10. You have nothing against women and think every man should own at least one.

11. You bathe at least monthly whether necessary or not.

12. You've ever had a crush on your neighbor's goat.

While in Greece, my wife had to go to a local dentist for dental work. She had one of the locals write the address on a card in Greek so she could get a taxi. At the same time the employee gave her verbal instructions as to where the office was located.

The guard hailed her a cab and she gave him the card with instructions. When the cab took off my wife noticed he was going in the wrong direction so she tried to get his attention and make sure he understood the address and directions. The cab driver kept ignoring her and motioned for her to sit back and be quiet. Frustrated, my wife stuck the card with the directions in his face and pointed to the address. The cab driver stopped, looked at the card and hit the top of his head with his palm and turned the cab around. He went back to the Embassy and reset his meter and then went on the correct address. Most of our experiences in Greece highlighted their honesty. It should be noted if a passenger tells a Greek cab driver to stop by a police officer, he will even though he knows he may face criminal charges.

During a TDY, my companion and I took a cab from our hotel. Upon leaving the cab my companion noted he had left his wallet on the seat. I stayed with our baggage while he went running down the road hoping to catch the cab in heavy traffic. Fortunately, a local citizen stopped and offered him a ride so they could catch the cab driver who knew the wallet was in the backseat but wouldn't stop. After chasing the cab for several blocks, they managed to catch him. The local citizen gave my companion a ride back. Outside of getting salmonella and being sick for a week, the rest of our TDY was uneventful.

The locals use three-wheel motorcycles with small carriages attached as a mode of transportation. It should be noted, if you try to get a bargain fare with these drivers, be prepared for a speed-demon ride to your destination. The drivers are in a hurry so they can dump you out and catch another fare. After the first ride, I paid extra.

During one of my TDYs, I was traveling with several companions through different countries. We had a day layover in Pakistan so we decided to go shopping. One of my companions knew of this fabulous rug dealer and insisted we go with him to buy a rug. He and my other companions bought rugs but I wasn't interested. The rug dealer felt he was not a good host if he did not sell me a rug at a giveaway price as a token of his friendship. It should be noted his shop was located in the Hilton Hotel—nothing is cheap there. Well to make a long story short I bought the rug at the giveaway price of $300. Later while browsing in the flea market, what do I see? An identical type rug selling for $100, negotiable.

While traveling with these same companions, we also stopped in

Egypt and stayed at the Holiday Inn next to the Pyramids. Two of my companions wanted me to go with them to visit the Pyramids and take pictures. I declined their offer and stayed in my room reading. After several hours they returned with the following tale:

When they got to the Pyramids, they started to take pictures. A camel driver came up to them and offered to let them take a picture on a camel in front of the Pyramids. After getting on the camel, they noticed the camel driver taking them into an isolated area away from other tourist. They questioned his motive and he indicated he wanted them to get a better site for a picture. After getting the pictures they asked how much for his service, he quoted $20 . . . *each.* They were upset over the price but were afraid to make a scene because they were isolated. So they paid the money and started walking back to the more populated area. As they were walking, an Arab driving a carriage stopped and offered them a ride. Being smarter now they wanted to know how much he charged before they got into the carriage. The drive said the ride was free as he wanted to show good will toward American. As they were riding he told them how much he likes Americans and hoped they were enjoying the sights. After a while, he asked if they would mind meeting his boss so he could make a favorable impression. They were happy to accommodate his request in return for such a pleasant ride in his carriage.

His boss had a big tent set up near the Pyramids. They were escorted into the tent where they were asked what they would like to have to drink. They declined as they were in a hurry to get back to the hotel. Well, the Arab boss reminded them he had asked them what they want to drink, not if they wanted a drink. This set the tone for what was to follow. It seems the boss wanted to show his hospitality by selling them, at giveaway prices, concentrated perfume mixes. The price was only $20 per one-ounce bottles. Again our adventurous travelers were isolated inside a tent where his reasonable offer was too good to turn down.

If there is a moral to these experiences, it is: in the Middle East, nothing in life is free.

The Agency places a high value on language expertise. Happily, I speak fluent Midwestern.

I'm writing a novel that will include a DI analyst named Christian Muhammad Shapiro: a belt-and-braces type without strong convictions who likes to hedge his bets.

My wife and I were assigned by our respective offices to participate in a three day symposium at an undisclosed Agency facility. Far be it for someone in one office in the DI to talk to another, especially because I was on the IC Staff, so we were each assigned a room. When I gave mine up, some clown suggested that it might be a first! Imagine—sleeping with one's _own_ spouse at an undisclosed Agency facility! *((No attribution, please!)) (Editor's note: This is CIA's equivalent of Henny Youngman's plea.)*

DCI William Casey decided to give a special award to the legendary Clarence "Kelly" Johnson, the former head of the Lockheed "Skunk Works" and the designer of the U-2 and the SR-71 aircraft. Kelly and his wife arrived at the appointed time for the ceremony that was held in the DCI's conference room. Kelly had agreed to speak afterward in the Auditorium. Those who were in the DCI's conference room proceeded to the entrance of the Auditorium. On the way all eyes were on Kelly, but upon arrival someone noted that Mrs. Johnson was not with the group. There was sudden panic when they realized that she was apparently lost somewhere in the

Headquarters building. A posse was dispatched to find her while the restless audience was wondering why the speaker had not arrived on time. Ten minutes or so passed and she was found wandering in a hallway while wondering why everyone had left her when she stopped for a restroom break. After an embarrassing delay, Mrs. Johnson arrived and Kelly proceeded to deliver an excellent talk to a packed Auditorium.

So much attention had been on Kelly that no one noticed what she had done. Next time, please don't forget to keep your eyes on the wife of the honored guest.

The walls and ceilings of the Original Headquarters Building were once honeycombed with a pneumatic tube system. Desk officers of a certain age throughout the building proudly display one of the tube system's artifacts on their desks. Before the advent of computer-mediated communication, the tube system permitted rapid sharing of draft cables and memos across the building's numerous offices. It was also a great medium for sending gifts, pranks, and foodstuffs. The closure of the tube system was lamented throughout Headquarters; it was replaced by a sprinkler system.

The six phases of a project
1. Enthusiasm
2. Disillusionment
3. Panic
4. Search for the Guilty
5. Punishment of the Innocent
6. Praise and Honors for the Non-participants

If you're going to break the rules, do it subtly. A hunter in

Virginia shot himself when he fell out of his tree stand. The nationally-syndicated Don and Mike show ran the story. Their show was very popular among Agency folk, including those in the Office of Security, who recognized the name of the injured hunter as a chronic leave-abuser who was out that day on a bogus excuse.

The air conditioner in a cube farm started leaking on an analyst's desk, destroying paper. Analysts pulled the molding that held the partitions together and suspended it from the ceiling, creating an aqueduct that diverted the dripping water. This gutter system did several loops around the ceiling of the large office, until it arrived to water a beloved office plant.

Further Reading

Clarridge, Duane R. *A Spy for All Seasons: My Life in the CIA*. New York: Scribner's, 1997.

Dulles, Allen. *The Craft of Intelligence*. New York: Signet, 1963.

Earley, Pete. *Confessions of a Spy: The Real Story of Aldrich Ames*. New York: Berkley Trade, 1998.

Gates, Robert. *From the Shadows: The Ultimate Insider's Story of Five Presidents and How They Won the Cold War*. New York: Simon and Schuster, 1996.

Goodrich, Austin. *Born To Spy: Recollections of a CIA Case Officer*. Lincoln, Nebraska: iUniverse, 2004.

Gostick, Adrian and Scott Christopher. *The Levity Effect: Why It Pays to Lighten Up*. New York: Wiley, 2008.

Hall, Roger. *You're Stepping on My Cloak and Dagger*. New York: W.W. Norton, 1957.

Holmes, W.J. *Double-Edged Secrets: US Naval Intelligence Operations in the Pacific During World War II* Annapolis, Maryland: Naval Institute Press, 1979.

Hood, William. *Mole—The True Story of the First Russian Spy to Become an American Counterspy* Washington: Brassey's, 1993.

Katz, Barry M. *Foreign Intelligence: Research and Analysis in OSS, 1942-45*. Cambridge: Harvard University Press, 1989.

Lathrop, Charles E. *The Literary Spy: The Ultimate Source for Quotations in Espionage and Intelligence*. New Haven: Yale University Press, 2004.

Luther, Jean M., James E. Turner, and United States Central Intelligence Agency Family Advisory Board *Spies, Black Ties and Mango Pies* College Station, Texas: Intaglio, Inc., 2004.

MacKenzie, Compton. *Water on the Brain*. 1933. Reprint, Penguin, 1959.

Muggeridge, Malcolm and Ian Hunter. *Chronicles of Wasted Time: The Infernal Grove*. Regent College Publishing, 2006 reprint.

Ranelagh, John. *The Agency: The Rise and Decline of the CIA*. Touchstone Books, 1987.

Riebling, Mark. *Wedge: The Secret War Between the FBI and CIA*. New York: Knopf, 1994.

Sileo, Tom. *CIA Humor*. Alexandria, Virginia: Washington House/Trident Media, 2004.

Smith, H. Allen. *The Compleat Practical Joker*. 1953. Reprinted New York: Doubleday, 1980.

Tenet, George J. with Bill Harlow. *At the Center of the Storm: My Years at the CIA*. New York: HarperCollins, 2007.

Wallace, Robert and H. Keith Melton with Henry Robert Schlesinger. *Spycraft: The Secret History of the CIA's Spytechs from Communism to al-Qaeda*. New York: Dutton, 2008.

Epilogue

The Things I've Seen
©1996 words and music by Tom McCluskey

I've traveled the world over, I can't count how many times
Bought myself some secrets, told a few lies
Plying the middle between war and peace
Got lots of stories nobody'd believe

The things I've said; the things I've done
Nobody'd believe the things I've seen

For your eyes only, words can never tell
Loose lips and sunken ships from here to hell
Seen some lunacy; I've had myself some fun
Took myself a risk or two and when the day is done

Nobody'd believe the things I've said
The things I felt; the things I've done

National treasure in a Heineken box
Stealing our measure and picking those locks
(And leave) The things I've said
The things I've done; the things I've seen

I've toasted some toasts; partied with kings
Wish I had a source to tell me what my future brings
Leave behind some memories of the places I've been
All the names and cases, I can't remember when

Nobody'd believe the things I said
The things I've done; the things I've seen
Nobody'd believe the things I said
The things I've done; the things I've seen